PHILOSOPHY AND RELIGION

IN COLONIAL AMERICA

PHILOSOPHY AND RELIGION
IN COLONIAL AMERICA

Claude M. Newlin
Michigan State University

GREENWOOD PRESS, PUBLISHERS
NEW YORK   1968

Reprinted with the permission of the
Philosophical Library, Inc.

First Greenwood reprinting, 1968

LIBRARY OF CONGRESS catalogue card number: 68-23317

MANUFACTURED IN THE UNITED STATES OF AMERICA

CONTENTS

Part I

Part II

v

PREFACE

The use of philosophy in religious writings of the colonial period is virtually confined to New England. For th's reason I have limited my study to that one area. On account of the homogeneous nature of the population and their religion, this region provides material for a coherent and unified historical study.

The colonial epoch is not, however, one undifferentiated block of time. Within this era there are really two periods. The first of these extends from the beginning to the second decade of the eighteenth century. The second period extends from that time to the end of the eighteenth century.

The philosophical thought of the earlier period is limited in scope. It has already been minutely explained by Perry Miller in two books: *The New England Mind: The Seventeenth Century* (1939), and *The New England Mind: From Colony to Province* (1953). Hence I have made my treatment of this period brief.

The second period is marked by the acceptance of the new science and philosophy and by the influence of some English liberal theologians of the eighteenth century. Because of these influences considerable doctrinal divergency developed. The story of the deviations from the traditional faith of the New England churches and of the defense of this faith I have attempted to recount rather fully.

Claude M. Newlin

Madison, New Jersey

ACKNOWLEDGMENTS

I am indebted to the Yale University Press for permission to use a large number of quotations from their edition of Jonathan Edwards' *Religious Affections* and *Freedom of the Will*. To the Columbia University Press I am indebted for permission to quote extensively from *Samuel Johnson, President of King's College, His Career and Writings*. Quotations from *Selections from Cotton Mather*, ed. by Kenneth Murdock, are used with the permission of Harcourt, Brace and World.

I am grateful to the officials and staffs of the following libraries for use of their collections of rare publications and for courteous assistance: American Antiquarian Society, Boston Athenaeum, Boston Public Library, William L. Clements Library (Ann Arbor, Michigan), and the libraries of Union Theological Seminary and Drew University.

For financial aid enabling me to visit these libraries I am indebted to the All-University Research Committee of Michigan State University.

For effectively encouraging my research on the religious thought of colonial New England I am grateful to Dr. Russel B. Nye, Professor of English, Michigan State University. The interest which many of my graduate students have shown in my project has been a significant source of encouragement.

My greatest obligation is due to my wife, Dorothy Hull Newlin, who has provided expert collaboration at every stage of my work.

CLAUDE M. NEWLIN

1

It is this philosophy which is the subject matter of this world's wisdom, that rash interpreter of the divine nature and order. In fact, heresies themselves are prompted by philosophy. . . . Wretched Aristotle! who taught them dialectic, that art of building up and demolishing, so protean in statement, so far-fetched in conjecture, so unyielding in disputes; self-stultifying, since it is ever handling questions but never settling anything. . . . Away with all projects for a 'Stoic,' a 'Platonic' or a 'dialectic' Christianity!

Tertullian (c. 160-240)

2

Thus philosophy was necessary to the Greeks for righteousness, until the coming of the Lord. And now it assists towards true religion as a kind of preparatory training for those who arrive at faith by way of demonstration.

Clement of Alexandria (c. 200)

PHILOSOPHY AND RELIGION
IN COLONIAL AMERICA

PART I

THE PURITANS AND THEIR PHILOSOPHY

By the time the Puritans migrated to New England they differed from the Anglicans in three different areas of religious thought: (1) church polity, (2) theology, and (3) philosophy.

It was in the realm of church polity that the Puritans differed most radically from those who were satisfied with the episcopalian organization of the Church of England. Without having any clear-cut program for church government when they came to New England, they soon worked out the Congregational system, in which the only authoritative unit of church authority is the individual congregation. There was no overhead authority, such as bishop or synod, with judicial authority to enforce decisions regarding matters of doctrine or discipline. Provision was made, however, for the maintenance of orthodoxy and good order by the use of church councils. These councils were not standing organizations representing a definite ecclesiastical region. They were called only when problems arose in individual churches and the delegates represented neighboring churches. On account of this loose term, considerable latitude could be exercised in the selection of the members of the councils. These councils had power to issue decisions in which ministers or congregations were advised or admonished, but these decisions were not binding and there was no means of enforcing them against the will of the individual congregations. This aspect of the congregational church order had great significance for the future of theology and philosophy in New England, which was the only area in the world where it was the established church order. In the early period the decisions of church councils were accepted, though they were not enforceable. Later, however, when liberal ministers were approved and supported by liberal congregations, there was no way of maintaining orthodoxy in all the churches. For this reason considerable doctrinal variety developed in the churches, including in some cases complete repudiation of the distinguishing features of the original body of doctrine. The congregational system thus eventually permitted the development of a situation in which a considerable amount of philosophy of one kind and another was utilized to support or attack theological doctrines.

Theologically the Puritans did not have much to quarrel with in the articles of the Church of England, and the New England church definitely approved the theological portion of the Westminster Confession, issued in 1643. Although the New England Puritans did not consider themselves to be literally disciples of John Calvin, yet their theology was basically Calvinistic, with some modification. Above all they emphasized the absolute sovereignty of God and hence the complete subordination and dependence of man. This conception of God seems to underlie the five points which were formulated at the Synod of Dort in 1619 and provide the most convenient summary of Calvinistic doctrine. The first and most important of these points is the doctrine of total depravity, or original sin. According to this doctrine, man's intellect, on account of the fall of Adam, was darkened and his will vitiated. This depravity could be eradicated only by an infusion of divine Grace, by which conversion or regeneration is effected. This conversion is not possible for all men, however.

2

According to the second of the points, which stated the doctrine of unconditional election, God had, before the creation, selected some men for salvation and others for eternal damnation. This election was unconditional because it was not contingent on foresight of any personal merit in the individual elected for salvation. This election without regard to possible virtue in the individual character was considered a necessary exercise of God's absolute sovereignty.

The salvation of the elect was not achieved without a change in their characters. This was not brought about, however, by their own initiative. According to the third point, covered by the term "prevenient and irresistible grace," the Holy Spirit operates upon the souls of the elect prior to and at the time of their regeneration in such a powerful way that the grace cannot be resisted.

The next doctrine is called "the perseverance of the saints." According to this, those who have been regenerated by the Spirit can never completely lose their sanctification. Since their regeneration was brought about by operation of the Spirit and not by their own efforts the effect is permanent. Otherwise, God's work might seem to be imperfect, and therefore his power could not be considered as unlimited.

The last of the points, called "limited atonement," is related to the doctrine of election. In opposition to the belief that Christ died for all who might qualify by faith and obedience, the atonement secured by the sacrifice of Christ was intended only for the elect.

The doctrines of election and grace brought up a problem concerning conduct. It was easy for some people to draw the conclusion that if the elect were assured of salvation, they did not need to do anything toward earning it by good works. The Puritans were, however, rigid moralists and thought that good works were obligatory. Since the regenerate had been sanctified, their sanctifi-

3

cation had to be manifested in their conduct. Good works were, therefore, not the cause but the evidence of regeneration and of justification.

The original Calvinism was somewhat modified in England by the concept of the "covenant." According to this idea, there was an agreement between God and the elect concerning the terms of salvation. This meant that both parties were bound by a contract. The effect of this was to place a definite responsibility on the individual Christian to live up to the agreement. And since God also had made promises which he was bound to honor, the exercise of his sovereignty could not be quite as arbitrary as it might otherwise have seemed to be.

In New England the concept of the covenant was also applied to other matters than the strictly theological. When congregations were formed the members signed a written covenant. All of New England was thought to be in a covenant with God and hence the people were considered to be under unusually binding obligations to be faithful to their professions. Ideas of government were also strongly affected by the concept of the covenant.

Although the professed interests of the early New Englanders were dominantly religious, their thinking was not all confined to or even determined by their theological doctrines. Their intellectual interests also included "humane learning" as it was known at the time. This "humane learning" was described and defended by Charles Chauncy, President of Harvard, in a commencement sermon entitled *God's mercy, shewed to his people in giving them a faithful Ministry and schools of Learning for the continued supplyes thereof*, delivered in 1655. This defense was needed, Chauncy thought, because an English writer, William Dell, had recently attacked liberal education on the grounds that the curriculum included the writings of pagans which often contained indecent matter.

4

In defining "humane learning" Chauncy said that it "may either be taken for all that learning that the heathen Authors or philosophers have delivered in their writings: or else all other Arts besides Theology, as they call *physicks, ethicks, politics* &c.: taken in also the grounds of languages, *Latin, Greek & Hebrew.*" In answer to Dell's objection to the use of the ancient classics, Chauncy said: "Now in the former sense, if *Mr. D.* do mean by humane learning, all that learning that the heathen men have uttered out of the light of nature: It will be a great oversight to pass such a sentence upon it. . . . There are certain principles of truth written even in corrupt nature, which heathen authors have delivered unto us, that do not cross the holy writ. . . . And who can deny but that there are found many excellent and divine morall truths in *Plato, Aristotle, Plutarch, Seneca* &c."

In defense of other subjects, Chauncy said: "But now if humane learning be taken in the second sense, for all those Arts that are commonly taught in Universities, as *Physicks, Ethicks, Politicks, Oeconomicks, Rhetorick, Astronomy* &c . . . , I will be bold to affirm, that these in the true sense and right meaning thereof are Theologicall & Scripture learning, and not to be counted as humane learning" (pp. 32-38).

Since the New England Puritans could read the ancient philosophers and moralists with profit and since theology itself could be conceived as comprehending all the arts taught in the universities, it is obvious that their thinking was not confined within the limits of Calvinistic theology.

The Puritans were not only privileged to make use of the philosophical writings of pagans but they had a philosophy of their own which included much that was outside the realm of Calvinistic theology.

The philosophical revolution which was a part of the

Puritan movement consisted in the repudiation of almost all of the Scholastic philosophy, a part of which was still utilized in the universities at the time when the Puritan ministers had been students. This change is illustrated by Cotton Mather's account of what had happened in the intellectual development of his grandfather, John Cotton. "But," Mather said, "although he had been Educated in the *Peripatetick* way, yet like the other Puritans of those times, he rather affected the *Ramaean* Discipline; and chose to follow the Methods of that Excellent *Ramus,* who like *Justin* of old, was not only a philosopher but a *Christian* and *a Martyr* also; rather than the more Empty, Trifling, Altercative Notions, to which the Works of the Pagan Aristotle derived to us, through the mangling Hands of the Apostate *Porphyrie,* have disposed his Disciples."[1]

The philosophy of Peter Ramus which the Puritans adopted was primarily a system of logic. Ramus had come to the conclusion that the Aristotelian logic as used in the universities and in theological writings was unnecessarily complicated. It was, he thought, an artificial fabrication, not based on either the nature of things or the natural operations of the human intellect. To replace the old logic Ramus devised a new system, first presented in *Dialecticae Libri Duo,* published in 1556.

In England the Ramean logic was utilized by William Ames in the composition of his *Marrow of Christian Divinity,* which was considered an authoritative work in New England. Ames not only used a new logical method in his theological reasoning, but he also rejected metaphysics as a distinct philosophical discipline. In this he was followed by the New England Puritans. In England also, John Milton wrote a textbook of Ramean logic.

In England the Ramean method was extended from logic to other subjects. The result of this was a compendi-

---

[1] *Johannes in Eremo,* pp. 52-53.

ous general survey of learning called "encyclopaedia" or "technologia." It was this "technologia" which supplanted metaphysics as a basic philosophical discipline. At Harvard *theses metaphysicae* gave place to *theses technologicae* after 1653, and henceforth technologia was an important part of the training at Harvard as it was later at Yale.

Technologia included a presentation of Ramean logic and of other arts treated in accordance with the Ramean method and in relation to each other. The logic of Ramus was based on two fundamental assumptions: (1) that the creation is an orderly structure, and (2) that the human intellect is so constructed that it more or less matches the structure of the world and can therefore understand it. This means that man can recognize as a self-evident truth any valid proposition pertaining to any aspect of the nature of things. Likewise, the falsity of propositions can be recognized. Since the mind operates by accepting or rejecting propositions, a technologia or encyclopaedia is a series of brief aphoristic statements classified and arranged in accordance with the structure of reality.

Although technologia was one of the most important formative influences in the training of students at Harvard and Yale until early in the eighteenth century, no American work of this type was published during the period. Outlines of learning were, however, drawn up by students. Of those which have survived in manuscript, the best was written at Yale in 1714 by Samuel Johnson.[1]

Later, looking back at the time when he wrote his outline, Johnson, after mentioning some of the old theological works used as authorities, said that "some few used to make synopses or abridgements of these scholastic systems" and that he himself "was thought to excel at

---

[1] Published from Johnson's Latin manuscript with English translation, in *Samuel Johnson . . . His Career and Writings*, by Herbert and Carol Schneider (New York, 1929), II, 55-185. All subsequent references to Johnson's writing are to this edition.

7

this, having drawn up a little system of all parts of learning then known." Since Johnson wrote this account long after he had repudiated the Ramean method, he added that his "little system" was "nothing else but a curious cobweb of distributions and definitions which only served to blow him up with great conceit that he was an adept" (I, 6).

He entitled his survey *Technologia sive Technometra* and further described it as an "Encyclopaedia, of Philosophy" and as a "System of Art."

"It is evident," Johnson said in a prefatory note, "that art has reflected its rays into the intellect of intelligent creatures ever since the most ancient times, and that therefore it has its reflected origin in the intelligent creature." To demonstrate, he gave a hasty survey of learning and philosophy down to "that great man Ramus." Richardson followed Ramus, "and then Ames, the greatest of them, followed him, and we follow Ames" (II, 61).

Johnson's system was, as he said, made up of distributions and definitions. He began with a generalized definition of art: "Art is the idea representing and directing *eupraxia*." Here the practical purpose of art is indicated, since *eupraxia* means well-doing. An idea is therefore considered as a pattern or representation of a thing and also, by means of this representation, as "directing *eupraxia* in action." "The effect which is produced by an agent and his *eupraxia* according to an idea is a *euprassomenon* —which on the other hand is the deed done." Hence art begins with an idea, followed by appropriate acting, and ends in a desirable accomplishment.

This general concept of art is applied in treating all the specific arts that are considered in the *Technologia*.

There are two kinds of art: archetypal and typal. The archetypal art, which is God's, is defined in the terms used in the general definition of art. "The archetypal art is the idea of things decreed in the divine mind which represents and hence directs the divine *eupraxia*. . . . The divine *eupraxia* is the art of God in creating, preserving, and governing his creatures. . . . The effect or *cuprattomenon* is the creature both as a thing created and as preserved and governed." The *euprattomenon*, or deed done, effected by *eupraxia*, or action, in execution of an idea is supposed to be good. In the case of the creation, "God saw what he had done and it was very good" (II, 65-67).

God's art is archetypal. Human arts are typal. "A typal art is an art which is a mere shadow of the archetypal art." While God's art is one single art of creation, human arts are varied. Of these there are two general types: entype and ectype. The first of these is based on the qualities of the various created things. Among the attributes of created things is value. Therefore, when we see that a thing "has value, we see it leading to a good end, to be made to the glory of the most great and good God, the Creator." This is the basis of "the *eupraxia* and rules of living" (II, 67-69).

The entypal art is based on the different specific attributes of different created things. Ectypal art is, on the other hand, "methodically constructed by universal rules" and is not concerned with the qualities pertaining only to special classes of things. The most general ectypal art is logic, which is defined as the "art of reasoning and arguing well." "Its object is the *eupraxia* of reason" (II, 69).

In his discussion of art Johnson had proceeded in accordance with the Ramean method. First he had given a general definition of art. Next he had divided art into two categories: archetypal and typal. Then he had divided typal art into two classes: entypal and ectypal. This statement of a proposition and the subsequent division into pairs of statements related to the original defi-

9

nition is the essential feature of the Ramean logic. The process of halving an idea and then subsequently halving the subsequent subordinate ideas is known as dichotomy.

The original work of Ramus had been simply a treatise on logic. In technologia, however, logic is presented as only one of several arts and is made subordinate to a generalized conception of art and its uses.

After defining logic and its function, Johnson stated the first of the dichotomies inherent in the subject: "the parts of logic are two—invention and arrangement" (II, 69).

The first part of the logical process, called invention, is "coming upon" or discovering an argument, not creating it. An argument is a topic or concept, not a disputation. The arguments that are based on one's own direct perception of facts are called "artificial," because they are supposedly formed in accordance with the rules of art. The truth of these arguments does not need to be demonstrated, since they "argue by their own force." Arguments are divided into two classes: "Primary and derivative." The primary are related to actual things, the derivative to the names of things.

Since things themselves are the source of primary arguments, their "effect on the argument is inherent in themselves and on their own account." From here on Johnson presented a complex series of definitions and distributions by dichotomy, only a few of which can be mentioned here as illustration. For instance, primary arguments are either simple or comparative. Simple arguments may either agree or disagree with each other. Those which agree may do so absolutely or after a certain manner. The absolute arguments include *causes* and things that are *caused*. The comparative arguments recognize likenesses and differences. In quantity, things may be equal or unequal. The unequal are larger or smaller. In quality, things are similar or dissimilar.

10

The second category of arguments is called "inartificial." These arguments are not derived from personal observation of the nature of things, but are based on the "testimony" of witnesses. The witnesses may be of two kinds: human or divine. Divine testimony is found in the Scriptures, which, being the Word of God, contain many truths which men themselves are unable to "invent" or discover. This particular aspect of the Ramist logic was of considerable value to the Puritan divines in their theological thinking.

The first part of the logical process, invention, is supposed to supply "arguments," or concepts. The concepts may or may not be true to fact, however.

The second part of the logical process is concerned with passing judgment on the arguments that have been arrived at by invention. In most manuals of Ramean logic this second division is called "judgment." Johnson, however, like Milton, preferred to call it "arrangement." Arrangement is, however, for the purpose of judgment. Arrangement is divided into two categories: axioms (or propositions) and syllogisms. The simpler matters can be presented in axioms. In these the arguments are arranged as subject and predicate of a proposition and are connected by a copula. They should be so arranged that the "relation of one to another is clear" (II, 85).

In the first part of the logical process the qualities of things are discovered. In the second part, the qualities of the statements about them are considered.

"The qualities of a proposition are primary or secondary." The primary are affirmative or negative. In the former the copula is "is"; in the latter, it is "is not."

The secondary qualities of a proposition are "truth and falsity." "A proposition is true when what ought to be joined is joined—and what ought to be separated is separated," and a proposition "is false when what

11

ought to be separated is joined and what ought to be joined is separated" (II, 87).

Not all truths, however, can be stated in easily judged axioms. In cases where a more complicated process might be required for the establishment of the validity of a proposition, the use of syllogistic reasoning might be necessary. Johnson, therefore, like other Ramist logicians, ended his presentation of logic with a rather long technical treatment of the syllogism.

After treating logic as the most general art, Johnson dealt with the elements of two "less general" ectypal arts: grammar and rhetoric.

"Grammar is the ectypal art of speaking well. Its object is the *eupraxia* of speaking. The *eupraxia* of speaking is the orderly procedure of the speaker in speaking" (II, 95).

"Rhetoric is the ectypal art of properly embellishing speech, or in other words, speaking with embellishment. Its object is the *eupraxia* of embellished speech or in other words to speak with embellishment" (II, 103-105). This treatment of rhetoric covers figures of speech, poetics, and the principles of oratory.

From the general ectypal arts, Johnson proceeded to the special. These are more special or less special. The less special, treated first, are arithmetic and geometry. "The object of arithmetic is the *eupraxia* of numbering" (II, 117). It is presented in a series of propositions classified as much as possible according to the principles of dichotomy.

"Geometry is the ectypal art of measuring well. . . . Its object is the *eupraxia* of measurement" (II, 121). Here again the presentation of the subject is according to the Ramean system of definition and distribution by dichotomy.

After the mathematical arts, which are classed as less

special, two more special arts are introduced. These are physics and theology.

Physics deals with the nature of objects and phenomena. The rejection of Aristotelianism by Ramus and his followers had not been complete. The medieval physics was retained, without the addition of any new knowledge. Johnson, therefore, like the other Rameans, simply presented the traditional physics in propositions distributed and arranged as much as possible according to the scheme devised by Ramus.

The second of the more special arts, and the final one presented in *Technologia,* is theology. As physics is concerned with the nature of things, theology is concerned with "the goodness in things." Goodness exists for the glory of God. And "since any action is always governed by the rules of art, and life is the noblest of actions and in it the goodness of the creature beams and shines forth, therefore, life may be directed by these rules." Theology is therefore defined, in terms of technologia, as "the ectypal art or doctrine of living for God." "Its object is the *eupraxia* of living for God. Living for God is following the will of God, living for the glory of God. . . ." Theology considered as an art "is expounded only on the basis of its object, the rules of living." These rules are "manifested by the examples and precepts revealed in Holy Scriptures."

The *eupraxia* of theology, which is living for God, is divided into two parts: faith and observance. Under the heading of faith, Johnson presented a long list of theological propositions, many of them supported by Scriptural texts. The doctrines are the ordinary Protestant doctrines of the time, stated and arranged according to the Ramean scheme.

The second part of the art of living for God is observance. Observance involves virtue and action according to virtue. Virtue is defined as "the state in which the will

13

is inclined toward well doing" and "an action according to virtue is an action flowing from a disposition to virtue" (II, 179). The two species of observance are religion and justice. Religion considered as observance includes worship and prayer, or duties toward God. These duties are prescribed in the first four of the ten commandments. Justice is "love of neighbor, which is the observance by which we observe our duty toward our neighbor." These duties are prescribed in the last six of the ten commandments, and pertain both to the neighbor's "person and his external goods" (II, 183).

Johnson's main title for his work was *Technologia* but he also described it as an *Encyclopedia of Philosophy*. He had begun with a generalized definition of art. After completing his treatment of theology, the highest of the arts, he added a definition of "Encyclopedia." "Encyclopedia is the circular comprehension of all the arts in the interest of the subordination of ends. . . . Its love is philosophy. Its knowledge is *pansophia*, since it is the knowledge of all things" (II, 185).

It is clear, however, that the Ramean system provided only a method of dealing with existing knowledge. It included no method for adding to the existing body of knowledge or of eliminating the errors contained in the traditional body of learning.

At the time when Johnson wrote his *Technologia*, however, the Ramean system had long been obsolete. Francis Bacon, in *The Advancement of Learning* (1605) had shown the futility of the Scholastic method of reasoning, as Ramus had done. The substitute he offered was, however, quite different from that of Ramus, since he proposed a method of the acquisition of new knowledge by observation and experimentation. The Royal Society had been founded in 1662 for the advancement of science. A revolution in physics had been effected by Sir Isaac Newton and in philosophy by John Locke. But none of this was known at Yale when Johnson wrote his *Technologia*. In his case, however, the situation was radically changed almost immediately after he completed his manuscript.

In Technologia, as represented by Johnson, theology was treated as one of the arts, although it was considered the highest and most important subject in the whole circle of sciences and arts. Religion was also, however, treated separately in accordance with the method used in handling all the subjects included in "technologia." The best example of expounding theology by this method is *The First Principles of the Doctrine of Christ; ... or the Doctrine of the Living God, wherein the Body of Divinity is Briefly and Methodically Handled* (1679), by James Fitch.

In praise of this method, Increase Mather, in a commendatory preface to Fitch's book, said "that those Models of Divinity . . . wherein Scriptural Definitions and Distributions, expressing the Sum of the only true Christian Religion, are methodically disposed according to the golden Rules of Art, have a peculiar excellency and usefulness attending them. In this way, that great and famous Martyr of France, *Peter Ramus,* held forth the light to others."

On account of Fitch's use of the Ramist method and of concepts embodied in "technologia," his presentation of Christian doctrine includes ideas that are not a part of the exclusively Calvinistic scheme.

Religion may be considered under two aspects. It "may be called an Art, as it consists of precepts, breathing the first and truest knowledge by which man is guided to his end, but it's called a Doctrine, because none can learn it but those who are taught of God." "None can learn it by the book of nature, for there are some lessons in Religion which are not to be found in the book of Creation, (namely) man's *Apostacy* and *Anastasie,* how at first man did

15

fall, and how he is recovered by Christ, and the book of nature is blurred by man's sin, the curse is fallen upon the works of Creation, and thus this book is darkened." "This can not be learnt only by humane industry, for man by nature is void of spiritual eye-sight." Religion is therefore "called a Doctrine" since "it is taught" by God. This teaching is done in two ways: "1. By giving the Rule from Heaven [revelation]. 2. By the illumination of the Spirit of God" (pp. 1-2).

Religion is defined as "a Doctrine of living unto God." It "consists of two parts, Faith and Obedience" (p. 1).

Faith, the first part of religion, "is a trusting in God for life, proceeding from a grounded knowledge of God as he hath made known himself in his sufficiency, and in his efficiency." Faith proceeds from "knowledge of God, for there can be no desire of an unknown God, no believing on him whom we do not know." Thus "Faith is wrought by knowledge" but "it is not knowledge nor properly any virtue of the understanding." "Life itself is its Object, hence happiness and goodness . . . and this is properly the Object of the will. . . . Hence this Faith is seated in the will" (p. 3).

Although faith is seated in the will rather than in the understanding, the achievement of faith is preceded by the exercise of reason. "Faith apprehends in the way of Reason, for God hath made man a reasonable Creature, —Reason,—hence Faith apprehends by Reason, otherwise man should go without his guide, and see with his sight, a portion of the beams of God, not the Sun in itself, not as God is in himself" (p. 4).

Since reason can achieve only an incomplete apprehension of divine things, it must be supplemented by faith. In showing the relationship between faith and reason, Fitch argued that it is similar to the relationship between reason and what is presented to the intellect by the senses. In explaining these relationships, Fitch employed the basic concepts of art utilized in "technologia."

"The act of Faith," he said, "is higher than the act of Reason, for Reason in man acts upon and is conversant about, only that Reason which shineth in divine Truth, but Faith is taken up with looking upon the divine goodness in them.

"Hence Reason in a believer is a means to let in light and goodness beyond Reason, that as the senses are means to present the Reason in things to the Reason in man, although the Reason is above Sense, so Reason is a means to present a divine good unto Faith, though that divine good is above Reason, but as Reason can use the *Prattomenon* of the Rule of Sense, (namely that which is effected by it, so Faith can use the *Prattomenon* of the Rule of Reason, that which is effected by it, and yet these are distinct arts and have distinct Objects, and distinct lights" (p. 4).

In the section of his book devoted to faith Fitch explained all the most important Protestant doctrines. Among these the Calvinistic doctrine of God's decrees particularly lent itself to treatment in terms of "technologia." The statement of the doctrine in the Westminster Confession is: "God from all eternity did, by the most wise and holy counsel of His own will, freely and unchangeably ordain whatever comes to pass." According to Fitch's explanation God follows the procedure common to all arts in conceiving and executing his decrees. "The Efficient causes of his decree [are] his wisdome and good will. 1. His wisdome . . . He acts well [*eupraxia*]. 2. Hence according to Rule. 3. This rule is not of the creatures but of him. 4. This rule by which he acts is [like the starting point in the practice of any of the arts] the idea or pattern of well acting. 5. This Idea in God is the first cause of well acting." God's "idea" is, however, unlike man's, since, "it borroweth not." The

17

effect of God's acting on "creatures" is an "imprinting" and "that wisdome in the creatures is imprinted, and is the expression or Image of" God's wisdom. "Hence the Rules of Art as in God are eternal, but as in the frame of Creation they are in time." Fitch hence concluded that "the definitions of things are eternal Truths, whatever becomes of the things themselves" (pp. 14-15).

Since faith, although partly depending on what is provided by reason, is beyond reason, the question remains as to how it is to be achieved. In accordance with Calvinistic doctrine, Fitch said: "It is wrought by unresistible power of the Spirit [irresistible Grace]." Those who are dead cannot themselves move "and all are dead by Nature." In fact, "Nature is," in essence, "resistance against the Spirit." The Spirit does not, however, grant the gift of faith without following a procedure. In answer to the question, "In what manner doth the Spirit work *Faith?*," Fitch gave an account of the effects wrought on the soul during the period when it is being made ready for the reception of Grace and the gift of faith. The Spirit prepares a man for faith by causing him to feel contrition, conviction of sin, compunction, and humiliation. It is only after these effects have been produced by the Spirit that the resistance of the natural man is overcome and Grace is irresistible (pp. 44 ff).

The doctrines of religion have been taught by God, since man in his fallen state is incapable of discovering them. These revealed doctrines are contained in the Bible. Hence the following question arises: "How do you prove the Holy Scriptures to be the Word of God?" (p. 57).

In answering this question, Fitch used the Ramist conception of artificial and inartificial arguments. Employing inartificial arguments, or arguments based on testimony rather than direct observation, he said: "The holy Scriptures are proved to be the word of God by the testimony of the godly in all ages, and by divine testi-

18

mony, the miracles wrought, and the testimony of the Spirit of God in the Saints . . . " (p. 57). The Scriptures are also proved to be the word of God "by many artificial arguments, because they do reveal divine wisdome, holiness, Justice, mercy, with most perfect harmony and wonderful efficacy, containing a perfect rule of Faith and obedience" (pp. 57-58).

In further elaboration of his argument, Fitch made a more distinct use of the Ramean method of dichotomizing. After saying that the "arguments" employed in proving the Scriptures to be the Word of God may be both artificial and inartificial he made a second division. The inartificial arguments are based on testimony of two kinds: human and divine. The human includes the "testimony of the godly in all ages." For instance, "in the primitive times, their preachers expounded these [the Scriptures]" (p. 57).

The divine testimony is found in the acts or action of God. It is, in turn, of two kinds: external and internal. The external is "by Miracles." The internal is "the Spirit of God in a believer witnessing" (pp. 58-59).

In presenting the "artificial arguments," Fitch showed that the Scriptures can be proved to be of divine origin because of the qualities and attributes that men may perceive in them. Since these qualities are perceived directly and are not learned by testimony, the arguments are artificial rather than inartificial. In his exposition of the qualities which men may see in the Scriptures, Fitch made use of the Ramean conception of invention. Although men may apprehend what is presented to them by the revealed Word, only God could "invent" the Scriptures. "1. They reveal wisdome above all the inventions of men, or Angels, the Mystery of the Trinity, and Man's Recovery . . . 2. Most beautiful holiness shining in these Scriptures. 3. Justice giving to God and man his due. 4. Most rich mercy. 5. Most perfect harmony,

19

though wrote by diverse, in diverse places and diverse languages . . . yet they all agree. 6. Their duration, 1. Were before other Writings. 2. Do continue and shall to the end of the World. 7. The Efficacy of them. 8. The perfection of them, they contain a perfect Rule of Faith and observance" (p. 59).

Fitch then argued that "either these Scriptures were invented by God or by some creature." They could not have been invented by a creature, for, if so, "it was either by some good or evil creature." It could not have been done "by some good creature for no good man or Angel would invent a thing and then say it was God's invention." It could not have been done "by some evil creature, for the holy Scriptures are contrary to the wicked." Fitch concluded that "therefore it is apparent these Scriptures are invented by God himself" (p. 59).

As has been seen, Fitch had dichotomized religion into two parts: faith and obedience. After devoting about three-fourths of his book to faith, he concluded with a brief discussion of obedience. Like religion as whole, obedience is dichotomized. In answer to the question, "How is obedience distributed?" Fitch said: "Obedience is distributed into love to God, and love to man, love to God being a respect to God, nextly as he is God, and may be called worship." The obedience which man owes to God is prescribed in the first four of the ten commandments, known as the first table. Answering the question, "What is that love to man the Law requireth," Fitch said, "The Law requireth to love thy Neighbour as thyself for the sake of God" (pp. 60-61). The duties in this category are prescribed in the last six of the ten commandments, known as the second table.

It seems clear that the religious thinking of the New England Puritans was broadened and enriched by their use of the Ramist logic and the "technologia" which grew out of it. Although these Puritans accepted the five

20

points of Calvinism the total body of their religious thought was not confined to these points or the consequences to be drawn from them. On account of the use of methods and philosophical conceptions that were not primarily derivatives of the Calvinistic "points," the "compleat body of divinity" of the New England Puritans might without too much exaggeration be described as Calvinistic humanism or humanistic Calvinism.

Although the Ramist logic and technologia had served a useful purpose, they had run their course by the early part of the eighteenth century. As has been observed in the discussion of Samuel Johnson, the methods and contents of "technologia" had been made obsolete by the advancement of science. In the field of learning in general, then, New England was due for a change. The same thing was true for the philosophical material utilized in theology. The New England divines of the seventeenth century had largely relied on the logic of Ramus for their conceptions of the operations of the human intellect. Early in the next century, however, as will be seen in later discussions of Samuel Johnson and Jonathan Edwards, the psychology of John Locke supplanted the logic of Ramus in situations where theological positions seemed to require philosophical support.

In other fields of thought also, there was a similar change. By the second quarter of the eighteenth century modern science, as represented by the work of Newton, Boyle, and others, had displaced much of the traditional learning which was incorporated in "technologia."

PART II

THE GROWTH OF RATIONALISM AND THE DEFENSE OF ORTHODOXY

I

The Dawn of the Enlightenment in New England

The first two decades of the eighteenth century saw the rapid development of interest in the New Learning in New England and the adoption of Newtonian physics and Locke's psychology. Equally important was the change in the intellectual atmosphere which became apparent in a heightened evaluation of reason, an increased regard for the Light of Nature and hence for Natural Religion, and the development of a broad-minded attitude known as "the Catholick spirit."

The most striking instance of sudden conversion to the New Learning was that of Samuel Johnson. As has been seen, the only books used at Yale when Johnson was a student there were those which had long been standard authorities to the Puritans. The New Learning was known to exist, but it was feared. Johnson said that at the time when he took his degree in 1714 the students had heard "of a new philosophy that of late was all the vogue and of such names as *Descartes, Boyle, Locke* and *Newton,* but they were warned against thinking anything of them, because the new philosophy, it was said, would soon bring in a new divinity and corrupt the pure religion of the country" (I, 6).

A change was soon to come, however. Johnson, as has been seen, said that the writing of his *Technologia* had served to "blow him up with a great conceit that he was adept, and in this pleasing imagination he continued a year or two." Then, "accidentally lighting on Lord Bacon's *Instauratio Magna,* or *Advancement of Learning* . . . he immediately bought it and greedily fell to studying it." "As," he said, "his thirst after knowledge and truth was always his ruling passion . . . he endeavored to keep his mind free from prepossessions and at liberty to consider the truth and right of the case on all occasions so that the reading and considering Lord Bacon soon brought down his towering imaginations." As a result, "he found himself like one at once emerging out of the glimmer of twilight into the full sunshine of open day" (I, 7).

Other modern English books also contributed to Johnson's conversion. In 1714 Yale received a gift of books from Jeremiah Dummer, agent for Connecticut in England. Thus, Johnson "had," he said, "all at once the vast pleasure of reading the works of our best English poets, philosophers, and divines, Shakespeare and Milton, etc., Locke and Norris, etc., Boyle and Newton, etc., Patrick and Whitby, Barrow, Tillotson, South, Sharp, Scot and Sherlock, etc. . . . All this was like a flood of day to his low state of mind" (I, 7). The effect of reading the philosophers and scientists was prompt and decisive. To the *Technologia,* which had been completed on November 14, 1714, he appended the following note: "And by next Thanksgiving, 1715, I was wholly changed to the New Learning" (II, 186).

As a result of reading the works of the Anglican divines, he was alienated from both Calvinistic theology and Congregational Church polity, and a few years later he and some of his friends were ordained as clergymen of the Church of England.

The most clearly apparent effect of the new learning, as revealed in his manuscripts of the next few years, is his adoption of Locke's psychology. In a short treatise on logic composed in 1720, he gave most of his attention to the process by which ideas are formed. At the beginning of his explanation of this process, he asserted, in Locke's terms, that "sensation and reflection are the origin of all our ideas and there are no ideas however so remote from them but what may be easily accounted for and referred to them" (II, 222).

After graduating, Johnson taught school at Guilford for two years. In 1716 he was appointed tutor at Yale and the next year a friend, Daniel Browne, who had also accepted the new learning, became a tutor there also. For a few years these two friends, both having the same point of view, constituted the total teaching staff of the college. Since they were dissatisfied with the traditional curriculum, they, as Johnson said, "joined their utmost endeavours to improve the education of their pupils by the help of the new lights they had gained." "They introduced the study of Mr. Locke and Sir Isaac Newton as fast as they could and in order to this the study of mathematics. The Ptolemaic system was hitherto as much believed as the Scriptures, but they soon cleared up and established the Copernican . . ." (II, 8-9).

One of the pupils who entered Yale the year Johnson began his work as a tutor was Jonathan Edwards, aged thirteen. Edwards, therefore, was introduced to modern ideas when he was very young and thus did not have to work his way out of the Ramean system as his tutors had done. There is no evidence in his writings that he was influenced by technologia. The impact of Locke on Edwards, however, was particularly strong. Samuel Hopkins, a disciple and his first biographer, said of

25

Edwards that he got more pleasure from it "than the most greedy miser finds when gathering up handfuls of silver and gold from some newly discovered treasure."

Under the stimulation of such reading, Edwards began his career as a thinker while he was a student at Yale. In a manuscript entitled *Notes on the Mind* he set down ideas on psychology, metaphysics, esthetics, moral philosophy, and natural philosophy which later appeared as key elements in his most important works.[1]

Beginning with a remark on perception, Edwards rapidly moved on to an assertion of the idealistic philosophy. Edwards thought that if we had only one sense, that of seeing, "we should not be as ready to conclude the visible world to have been an existence independent of perception, as we do." The ideas we acquire through the other senses, such as feeling, "are as much mere ideas, as those we have by the sense of seeing." "It is," Edwards explained, "now agreed upon by every knowing philosopher, that Colours are not really in the things, no more than Pain is in a needle; but strictly nowhere else but in the mind." In other words, since we know color as such only as a mental experience, it exists only in the mind, and so it is with all other sensations. Nothing then exists outside of the mind except "Resistance, which is Solidity." All bodies, however, are limited areas of resistance or solidity, and so there is "termination of this Resistance at the surface of bodies." This termination of resistance is the real nature of what is known as the "Figure" of bodies. These areas of resistance, or bodies, can be communicated from space to space, however, and this is known as Motion. Figure and motion are, however, nothing but modes of resistance, and not essential features of it. Where there is nothing to resist, there is, of

---

[1] All quotations from *Notes on the Mind* are taken from Clarence H. Faust and Thomas H. Johnson, *Jonathan Edwards: Representative Selections* (New York, 1935) pp. 27-37.

course, no resistance. Basically, then, "there is nothing but the Power of Resistance." Resistance itself "is nothing else but the actual exertion of God's power" and therefore "the Power can be nothing else, but the constant Law or Method of that actual exertion."

Edwards had spoken as if resistance, unlike colors, for example, existed outside the mind, and had explained resistance as "the exertion of God's power." He now, however, stated that it is easy to conceive of resistance as "a mode," that is, a possible but not essential feature of an idea. Hence, any idea such as a color may be resisted—"it may move, and stop and rebound." "The world is therefore," Edwards concluded, "an ideal one; and the Law of creating, and the succession of these ideas is constant and regular."

Edwards understood that this ideal philosophy might make the supposedly exterior world seem completely insubstantial and not an object for scientific study. He insisted, therefore, that his principles did not "at all make void Natural Philosophy," which he defined as "the science of the Causes or Reasons of corporeal changes." He had already said that "the Law of creating, and the succession of these ideas is constant and regular." Because this constancy and regularity are due to God's activity, the study of the "reasons of things in Natural Philosophy" is really the study of God's constant way of acting. For all practical purposes, then, in relation to natural philosophy the "case is the same . . . whether we suppose the world, only mental, in our sense, or no." For scientific purposes, then, Edwards thought, "Though we suppose, that the existence of the whole of the material Universe is absolutely dependent on Idea, yet we may speak in the old way, and as properly, and as truly as ever."

Then, in a passage which combines both a religious and a mechanistic view, Edwards declared: "God, in the beginning, created such a certain number of Atoms, of such a determinate bulk and figure, which they yet maintain and always will, and gave them such a motion, of such a direction, and of such a degree of velocity; from whence arise all the Natural Changes in the Universe, forever, in a continued series.''

In Edwards' later writings, definite traces of the idealistic philosophy are infrequent. It seems probable, however, that it is implicit though intangible in his more mature writings. His concept of the world as a series of events which had been initiated by God and from which there could be no deviation and his concern with causation were later applied to both the natural and the moral worlds and, in a theological context, of fundamental importance in some of his most significant work.

The source of Edwards' idealism is unknown, since it cannot have come from any books to which he is known to have had access at the time. It seems likely that, having adopted Locke's conception that ideas originate in sensations produced on the mind by outside influences, he proceeded to the conclusion that the ideas in the mind are the actual reality and that they are produced not by the impact of a material world on the mind but by the direct action of God. The reason for Edwards' idealistic interpretation of what he got from Locke probably lies in the element of mysticism, which, as his ''Personal Narrative'' shows, was a part of his personal character.

From metaphysics and natural philosophy, Edwards, in writing these *Notes,* passed on to esthetics which he discussed in a note entitled ''Excellency,'' and moral philosophy, which he discussed in a note entitled ''Excellence.''

In speculating about the nature of beauty, Edwards was, whether he knew it or not, in line with earlier Puritan thought. Their concept of beauty had been related to their concept and high evaluation of order in the creation and in society. "It was Order," William Hubbard had said in 1676, "that gave Beauty to this goodly fabrick of the world, which before was but a confused Chaos. . . ." And with reference to a product of human skill, he had said, "In a curious piece of Architecture, that which first offers itself to the view of the beholder, is the beauty of the structure, the proportion that one piece bears to another, wherein the skill of the Architect most shows itself."

Although Edwards' theme in this note was excellency in general, he gave special attention to the nature of beauty. "There has been nothing more without a definition, than *Excellency*," he said, "although it be what we are more concerned with, than any thing else whatsoever." "But," he asked, "what is this Excellency? Wherein is one thing excellent, and another evil; one beautiful, and another deformed?" In his reading Edwards had somewhere encountered the idea that "all Excellency is *Harmony, Symmetry,* or *Proportion.*" Although he accepted this, he was dissatisfied because, he thought, previous writers had not explained *why* excellence lies in these qualities, and he therefore undertook to provide an explanation. He began with the statement that *"Equality, or Likeness of Ratios"* is the essential feature of pleasing objects. To illustrate this he pointed out that two equal circles or globes placed side by side have "more beauty than if they were unequal." Likewise parallel lines, because of the equality of distance between them, are more pleasing than oblique lines. "This simple equality . . . is," Edwards said, "the lowest kind of Regularity, and it may be called Simple Beauty."

Higher than this simple beauty, characterized by mere equality, is complex beauty which allows for inequalities. There must, however, be proportion among the elements of a complex pattern. Among the simple illustrations of

29

this point, Edwards considers a row of four dots, not all of which are the same distance apart. The first two are two inches apart, and the third is one inch from the second, half of the distance of the second from the first. To preserve proportion in the series, the fourth dot is placed one-half inch from the third. Thus, in spite of inequality, symmetry is maintained by the presence of proportion. In any object having complex beauty, equality of proportion rather than simple equality is to be found, although, Edwards said, "the Equalities in a beauty in any degree complicated, are so numerous that it would be a most tedious piece of work to enumerate them." In the beauty of "Flowers, vines, plants, trees, the bodies of men and animals," there is "a very complicated harmony." Not only is there proportion in objects, but also "in all natural motions . . . of bodies in the Universe . . . and therein is their beauty." Also there is harmony in music because of "the proportion which the several notes of a tune bear, one among another," although in this case the proportion is actually "in the particular vibrations of the air which strike upon the ear."

Having described the nature of beauty, Edwards was now ready for a reply to the previously unanswered question: "Why Proportion is pleasant to the mind, and Disproportion unpleasant." His solution is on an ontological basis. "Being," he said, "is nothing else but Proportion." "Disproportion, or Inconsistency" is, therefore, "contrary to Being." This inconsistency is a contradiction of the very nature of "Being" and hence is intolerable to anyone who perceives it, while, on the other hand, harmony with "Being" is "most pleasing."

Having worked his way from simple lines and dots up through complicated objects of nature, and to a consideration of the nature of being, Edwards was ready to give as a "universal definition of Excellency: *The Consent of*

Being to Being, or Being's Consent to Entity." This
"consent" he defined somewhat more intelligibly in a
later work as meaning "adjusted in the universal
system."

In this discussion of "Excellency" in material objects
Edwards had remarked that "Spiritual harmonies" are
of vastly greater extent than the harmonies in material
things. These spiritual harmonies are the subject of his
note entitled "Excellence."

In speaking of "Excellence in Bodies," Edwards had
been obliged "to borrow the word, *Consent,* from spiritual things." "There is no other proper consent," he
said, "but that of *Minds,* even of their Will; which when
it is of Minds towards Minds, it is *Love,* and when of
Minds toward other things, it is Choice. Wherefore all
the Primary and Original beauty or excellence, that is
among Minds, is Love." "Wherefore," Edwards concluded, "all Virtue, which is Excellency of minds, is
resolved into *Love to Being;* and nothing is virtuous or
beautiful in Spirits, any otherwise than it is an exercise,
or fruit, or manifestation, of this love; and nothing is
sinful or deformed in Spirits, but as it is the defect of,
or contrary to these."

These ideas about excellence in both things and souls
were not mere youthful fancies. They appear again years
later as essential features of some of his most mature
works.

In Massachusetts the shift to the new philosophy was
more gradual, possibly because at Harvard modern science had been gradually integrated with the traditional
learning.

The leading champion of modern science in Massachusetts was Cotton Mather. In 1712, while the new science
was still proscribed at Yale, Mather had called Newton
"the perpetual Dictator of the Learned world in the
Principles of Natural Philosophy" and "The most Vic-

torious Assertor of an Infinite *God,* that hath appeared
in the bright Army of them that have driven the baffled
Herd of Atheists away from the Tents of Humanity."[2]

Mather's interest in science in relation to religion soon
became more generalized, however. In this, he followed
the lead of some English writers who represented a
school of thought known as physico-theology. Of this
school of thought the most notable examples are John
Ray's *Wisdom of God Manifested in the Works of Creation* (1691) and William Derham's *Physico-Theology*
(1713). The aim of these and other similar works, as is
indicated by Ray's title, was to describe the phenomena
of nature in such a way as not only to demonstrate the
existence of God but to arouse a sense of wonder at God's
intelligence and ingenuity as it is revealed in the intri-
cacies of nature. Although the aim of these books is
religious, much more space is given to the description
of things in nature than to the religious conclusions
drawn from consideration of them. From the books of
Ray and Derham, and other scientific works, Mather
drew the material for *The Christian Philosopher,* published in 1721.

The significance of this book lies in the point of view
expressed in prefatory statements rather than in information contained in the main body of the work. The
preface is entitled "Religio Philosophica" [i.e., Philosophic, or scientific, religion], and the book is described
as "A Commentary, of the more Modern and Certain
Philosophy, upon that construction." This means, of
course, that modern science, being more exact than the
traditional science, was more useful for religious purposes. In stating his purpose more fully, Mather said:
"The Works of the Glorious GOD in the *Creation* of the
World, are what I now propose to exhibit: in brief

---

[2] Perry Miller, *The New England Mind: From Colony to Province* (Cambridge,
Massachusetts, 1953), p. 440.

32

Essays to enumerate *some of them,* that He may be glorified in them . . . *Chrysostom,* I remember, mentions a *Twofold Book of* GOD; the Book of the *Creatures,* and the Book of the *Scriptures*: GOD having taught first of all us by his *Works,* did it afterwards . . . by his *Words.* We will now for a while read the *Former* of these Books, 'twill help us in reading the *Latter.* They will admirably assist one another."

Further declaring his expectations in the "Introduction," Mather said: "The Essays now before us will demonstrate, that *Philosophy* is no *Enemy,* but a mighty and wondrous *Incentive* to *Religion*; and they will exhibit that PHILOSOPHICAL RELIGION, which will carry with it a most sensible *Character,* and victorious *Evidence* of a *reasonable Service."* Mather was perhaps more interested in stimulating a pietistic and charitable spirit than in producing intellectual conviction. He hoped his work would serve the cause of "GLORY TO GOD IN THE HIGHEST, and GOOD-WILL TOWARDS MEN . . . and a Spirit of *Devotion* and *Charity."*[3]

Admitting that he had derived most of his material from Ray and Derham, Mather said regarding his own contribution, "There is very little, that may be said, really to be performed by the Hand that is now writing; but only the *Devotionary Part* of these Essays." . . . He hoped that "if the *Virtuoso's,* and all the *Genuine Philosophers* of our Age, have approved the Design of the devout RAY and DERHAM, and others, in their Treatises; it cannot be distasteful unto them, to see what was more *generally hinted at* by those Excellent Persons, here more *particularly carried on,* and the more *special Flights* of the true *Philosophical Religion* exemplified."

As an example of Mather's "devotionary part," which was frequently exclamatory in style, the conclusion of

---

[3] Passages from *The Christian Philosopher* are quoted from Kenneth B. Murdock, *Selections from Cotton Mather* (New York, 1926), pp. 285-292.

his chapter on magnetism may be cited: "But what Great KING is He, who is the Owner, yea, and the Maker of all the *Magnets in the World! I am a Great* KING, *saith the Lord of Hosts,* and my Name is to *be feared among the Nations!* May the *Loadstone* help to carry it to them."

Mather's enthusiasm for the new science was forcefully expressed again in 1726 in *Manuductio ad Ministerium,* a book of advice for students preparing for the ministry. Part of the advice is of a pietistic nature and part of it relates to studies. The section devoted to studies covers both theology and the arts and sciences. In this part of his advice Mather relegated some of the traditional subjects to a very minor position, and elevated the new science to a major position.

"Instead of Squandering away your Time, on the RHETORIC," he said, " . . . my Advice to you, is, That you observe The Flowres and Airs of such *Writings,* as are most in Reputation for their *Elegancy"* (p. 34).

"Nor," he declared, "can I encourage you to spend very much Time, in that which goes under the Name of LOGIC." He had, he said, come to feel "a Contempt of the *Vulgar Logic,* learnt in our Colleges." He was sure that "those *Masters of Reason* . . . who . . . make the most *Rational Researches* into the true State of Things . . . rarely trouble their Heads to recall the *Old Rules* which they have recited unto their Tutors." The end of "all *syllogizing,"* he thought, "is only to confirm you in a *Truth* which you are already the Owner of." To appease defenders of the old discipline, however, the student should "go dip into your Logic." This "dip" would merely mean reading some one elementary treatise such as Milton's. Although Mather had come to see the futility of the Ramean logic taught in the New England colleges, he, unlike Johnson and Edwards, rejected Locke also. "For some Reasons," he said, "I would be excused from recommending an *Essay of Humane Understanding,* which is much in vogue'' (pp. 35-36).

"What I say of Logic," Mather continued, "I say of Metaphysicks." After reluctantly recommending the reading of one or two elementary treatises on metaphysics, he asked, "But then to weave any more *Cobwebs* in your Brains; to what Purpose is it?" (p. 37).

"As for ETHICS," Mather said, after admitting that there is such a thing as Christian ethics *"which cannot be spoken against,* yet of *That* whereon they employ the *Plough* so long in many Academies, I will venture to say, 'tis a *Vile Thing."* The trouble with this ethics is that "It pretends to give you a Religion without a CHRIST, and a *Life* of PIETY without a *Living Principle;* a *Good Life* with no other than *Dead Works* filling of it." Mather was willing to recommend the reading of one book in this field, however, since, he said, "It is not amiss for you, to know what this *Paganism* is" (pp. 37-38).

When Mather had graduated from Harvard in 1678, the commencement programs included theses in technologia, logic, grammar, rhetoric, mathematics, and physics. Now, in his advice to students he ignored technologia completely. Instead of mentioning grammar as an abstract subject, he gave advice about the study of Greek, Latin, Hebrew, Syriac, and French. Rhetoric he found useless with reference to the formation of style. Logic and metaphysics he found to be useless for the purpose of the advancement of learning. Mathematics he recommended highly. The physics which he could have learned at Harvard was now useless.

Having shown the sterility of some of the old disciplines, Mather declared: "What we call NATURAL *philosophy,* is what I must encourage you to spend much more Time in the Study of." Respecting the view of the physico-theology which had been the theme of *The Christian Philosopher,* he asserted: "Do it, in the continual

35

Contemplations and agreeable *Acknowledgements* of the
Infinite GOD, whose Perfections are so display'd in His
Works before you, that from them, you cannot but be
perpetually ravished into Acclamations of, *How Great
is His Goodness and His Beauty!*"

"Do it, with a *Design* to be led into those *Views* where-
with you will in Ways most Worthy of a *Man* effectually
Show yourself a Man, and may . . . answer the main END
of your Being, which is, To Glorify GOD; and therein
also Discharge the Office of a *Priest for the Creation* . . ."
(p. 47).

Emphasizing his support of the new science, Mather
declared, "When I said, *Natural Philosophy,* you may be
sure, I did not mean, the *Peripatetic.*" "It is indeed amazing," he said, "to see the Fate of the Writings which go
under the Name of *Aristotle.*" A contemptuous account
of the development and spread of Aristotelianism followed. With reference to Aristotle and the Catholic
Church, Mather said, "With the *Vile Person* that made
himself the Head of the Church at *Rome,* this Muddy-
headed Pagan *divided the Empire* over the Christian
World." Even the Saracens and Jews had embraced
Aristotelianism. Mather observed, "And tho' *Europe
has,* with fierce and long Struggles about it, begun to
shake off the shackles, he does to this Day . . . continue
to Tyrannize over the Humane Understanding in a great
Part of the *Oriental World.*" "No Mortal else ever had
such a Prerogative to *Govern Mankind,* as this *Philosopher*; who after the prodigious Cartloads of Stuff, that
has been Written to explain him . . . he yet remains in
many . . . Things . . . sufficiently *Unintelligible,* and forever in almost all things *Unprofitable.*" After thus dismissing Aristotelianism as being useless and some recent
speculations, some of them based on *Genesis,* as interesting but unreliable, Mather said to the student, "And
therefore, as thorough an Insight as you can get into the

36

Principles of our *Perpetual Dictator,* the Incomparable Sr. *Isaac Newton,* is what I mightily commend unto you." But it was not only Newtonianism that Mather commended. "Be sure," he said, "The *Experimental Philosophy* is that in which alone your Mind can be at all established." For this purpose he recommended reading the *Transactions* of the Royal Society, the writings of Boyle and other scientists, and "what has been communicated by our Industrious *Ray,* and our Ingenuous *Derham,* who still nobly serve *Religion* as well as *Philosophy.*" At greater length, and with somewhat more enthusiasm, he also recommended another recent book. "And," he said, "whatever it might be for *me* to say so unto any One else, I hope, it will be no Indecency for me to say it unto *you*; that if you desire to see the largest Collection, I have yet seen of the *Discoveries* which the last Age has made in *Philosophy,* adapted unto the general Capacity of Readers; and short Essays upon every Article, to Show and Raise those Dispositions of PIETY, wherein the Works of the Holy and Blessed GOD invite us to Live unto Him . . . you have this prepared for you in a Book Entituled, THE CHRISTIAN PHILOSOPHER."

Although Mather dropped a strong hint that he was the author of this book, he modestly refrained from actually giving his own name. The title of the work was, however, printed in the bold-faced capitals usually reserved for GOD and CHRIST.

In a warning to his readers, however, Mather said, "And above all, I would have you see to it, that you be not, like some haughty, and short-sighted, and half-witted, *Smatterers in Philosophy,* be seduced into the *Folly* of doubting the *Existence* or *Providence* of a Glorious GOD, by a Study, which, if well-pursued, would *Compel you to Come in* to a *Strong Faith,* wherein you would *give Glory* to Him, on all Occasions" (pp. 47-51).

In *The Christian Philosopher* Mather had made a religious use of a large number and variety of the objects and phenomena of nature. He now gave a religious interpretation of the view of the world-order made possible by modern science, especially by Newtonianism. First quoting from another writer the statement *That as the World was at first Created, so it has been ever since preserved, by the Immediate Hand of God,* he continued, elaborating on this theme: "You will see, That the Influences of one thing upon another in the *Course of Nature* are purely from the Omnipotent and Omnipresent GOD, actually forever at Work, according to his own *Laws,* and putting His *Laws* in Execution, and as the *Universal Cause* producing those Effects, whereof the *Creatures* are but what One may call, *The Occasional Causes.* You will also be often and quickly carried up into those *Immechanical Principles*, from whence, *The next step is into* GOD." Using Newton for an example of "Immechanical Principles," he said: "The *Gravitation* of Bodies is One of them; for which *No Cause* can be assigned, but the *Will* of the Glorious GOD, who is the *First Cause* of all" (p. 52).

The earlier Puritans had, as has been seen, been strongly impressed by a sense of order in the creation. Newton's precise formulation of the law of gravity and of the laws of motion, to which Mather had access, gave the concept of order a quite new content. The earlier Puritans had also operated with the Aristotelian concept of first and second causes. The vaguely defined or un-defined second causes were, however, a quite different matter from the laws which had been precisely formulated by Boyle and Newton.

Later in the century this precise definition of laws of nature led to a mechanistic conception of the universe which was the basis for a scientific deism, represented by Tom Paine, which repudiated Scripture as revelation altogether. Mather had not, as has sometimes been said, become a half-way deist on account of his acceptance of Newtonianism. Basically he was still faithful to the Calvinism of the New England tradition.

Mather was the only one of the clergymen of Massachusetts who championed the new science vigorously. By the time he published the *Manuductio* in 1726, however, the new ideas were apparently rather widely accepted. In that same year Thomas Prince and Joseph Sewall, ministers of the Old South Church, wrote a preface for Samuel Willard's *Compleat Body of Divinity* in which they explained the theological merits of the book. Since Willard had completed his book in 1707, however, some kinds of thought had changed, and this also they explained. "Some Readers indeed," they said, "may find the Author less exact in his *Philosophical Schemes & Principles,* which happen to be of a more ancient Date, and not so suited to the Opinions reigning at the present Age. In anticipation of which we need only observe, that in such things as these every Person is entirely left to his Freedom without Offense; that the internal Nature of Things being so extremely incluse and hidden *many* of our *Philosophical Schemes* have been but mere *Hypotheses* subsisting only in the Imagination of Men; and being unsoundly rais'd from a few imperfect Observations of the Appearances & Events of Nature, have been successively thrown out by *others* as unstable as they; and that our Author chiefly flourish'd when we were just emerging out of those Obscurities."

In 1727, the year after Mather's *Manuductio* and the preface of Prince and Sewall were published, the ministers of New England were provided with an opportunity to consider the relations between science and religion. For many years the ministers had made use of natural disasters as occasions for sermons in which the people were told that they were being warned or punished because of their sinfulness or indifference to their religious obligations. An earthquake which occurred in Boston on November 19, 1727, now provided such an occasion. Of the many admonitory sermons which were preached on account of this earthquake, one of the most important with reference to the relations between science and religion is *The Voice of the Lord from the Deep Places of the Earth,* delivered to the legislature by Thomas Foxcroft, minister of the First Church of Boston.

In words reminiscent of Mather's *Christian Philosopher,* Foxcroft said: "As the Works of Nature & Grace, so the Works of Providence, are to be seriously consider'd by us, if we would show ourselves Men . . . The works of the Lord are great; sought out of all Them that have Pleasure therein. Remember then that thou magnify his Works which Men behold." "To consider them indeed in their Essence and natural Causes & Properties, is," he said, "not so much the Business of the Christian as the Philosopher." "But," he added, "the same things which are the Subjects of *Philosophy,* do under different Respects, as they are referred to their Efficient, and Final Cause, also come into Consideration in Divinity."

Illustrating this point more specifically, Foxcroft, using the language of physico-theology, said: "The Laws of *Gravitation* and *Magnetism,* and the Law of *Instinct.* those mysterious Contrivances of His infinite Wisdom, are established in the World by his Almighty Hand; by which Means the several Parts of the Earth afford their various Productions for the Support & Service of its Inhabitants, in their innumerable Species, and with a most surprising Harmony all Things conspire to serve the particular Purposes they were made for, which terminate in the Benefit of the Universe and the Glory of the Creator."

Foxcroft then described, in what he supposed to be a

scientific manner, the characteristics of the earth which make earthquakes possible. "Philosophy," he said, "teaches us to suppose that the Earth is not a perfectly solid Body, but has mighty *Caverns* within it, and innumerable lesser *Veins* and hollow Spaces; where are Fountains of Water, or Treasures of Winds and Vapours. And the whole Globe is filled with vast Stores of Fire and combustible materials. These appear to be the Provisions in Nature for those terrible Convulsions the Earth is sometimes thrown into." Although these natural conditions, in a certain way, account for earthquakes, still "the Lord of Hosts is the grand EFFICIENT."

Foxcroft granted that "doubtless in ordinary Cases at least, there are natural Causes of this *Phaenomenon*." "But yet," he said, "the most critical Inquirers into Nature are at a loss how to account for the generating of the Earthquake, and the Operations of it, without ascribing a great deal to the more immediate Influence of some supernatural Power. . . . It seems truly to be a more immediate Act of Providence, than most other Events" (pp. 22-23).

Since "the Earthquake is an eminent Demonstration of the Divine Power and Presence: So it is usually a Token of *Wrath* kindled against a Place for the Wickedness of them that dwell therein" (p. 25). On this basis, then, Foxcroft delivered this exhortation to the members of the legislature: "May the Terror of the *Earthquake* immediately awaken all in places of Power, from an affecting view of the great Necessity of a Reformation, to labour the Subduing of the many provoking Evils, which make the Land tremble!" (p. 40).

It was not only in new knowledge that the new period differed from the preceding. This is particularly apparent in a heightened regard for human reason and the light of nature. In some cases this led to a highly favor-

41

able estimate of Natural Religion, which was founded on a philosophical rather than on a Scriptural basis.

Near the end of the preceding period, Samuel Willard, in his *Compleat Body of Divinity*, had stated the traditional New England view of man's reason. "Man knocked his head in his fall," he said, "and craz'd his understanding, as to divine Truths. It is but little he knows of that Rule. Some broken Fragments, and moth-eaten registers, old rusty outworn monuments there are; but so imperfect & illegible, that there are but very few of them, that he can spell out what they mean; and in others he is mistaken. For this reason, a State of Nature is called a State of *Darkness*, and natural man said to be brutish."

One of the ministers who represented, in a moderate way, the new and higher evaluation of reason was Benjamin Colman, minister of the Brattle Street Church. In a sermon entitled *A Humble Discourse on the Incomprehensibleness of God*, delivered in 1715, Colman dealt mainly with man's inability to understand wholly either God's ways in nature or His ways in working on the souls of men. Nevertheless, he insisted that man has a capacity to arrive at religious truths. "No Man that will use his Senses, and observe the Heavens and the Earth, can without forfeiting his Reason . . . Worship a *Stock and Stone* . . . ; for if he will but think he must easily know that all these things have some Glorious *Maker*, whose Creature he himself is also, and *Whom* only he must therefore Worship. If a *Heathen* will not thus use his Reason, he *despises his Maker*, and dishonors his own Nature . . . " He can be held guilty if he thus fails to use his reason and also if he violates his conscience, because, Colman said, "The Law of *Nature* is a very *Sacred* Law, and the Light of Nature a very *great Light*." To Colman, apparently, "a state of Nature" was not "a state of *Darkness*" as it had been to Willard.

In 1723, in another sermon, the main purpose of which

was stated in the title *God Deals with us as Rational Creatures,* Colman did not consider reason primarily as a means of discovering religious truth, but rather as a faculty through which God works in leading man to repentance. In his exposition he gave this account of the nature of man. "The faculties of our Souls are to us as the clearest looking-glass wherein to see GOD." "There is a Soul in man endued with a principle and power of reasoning." However, "this mind needs to be enlightened by the Spirit of GOD." Although even "in our *natural* state we are taught more than the beasts of the earth..."; in *Regeneration* the Understanding of man is divinely Illuminated from above to discern the things of GOD" (p. 4). He then quoted the text: "The Spirit of Man is the Candle of the Lord"—a text which was frequently cited in eighteenth-century New England by ministers who placed a high value on reason.

Explaining the original and later status of reason in man, Colman said: "Our holy and glorious Maker *has written his Law in us; and it was written very fairly in man at first.* Yes, there yet remains very legible upon the heart of man much of the will and law of GOD to him... and he that will but . . .attend to the voice of his own Reason and Conscience, can't but read it there" (p. 5). "Indeed, this is *essential* to a rational Creature to have the *Law of* GOD written on his mind and Conscience; for Reason in us is this Law; and it is given man for his Government and Conduct" (p. 6).

Although Colman had said that, in spite of the fall, "there yet remains very legible upon the heart of man much of the will and law of *God,*" he considered that this was insufficient. Therefore, "since our fall GOD has written his Law, mind and will to us in his Word. This became necessary for the *recovery* of man from the Ruin his Apostacy had bro't upon him. The light of reason was wofully *obscured,* and the law written upon his heart dreadfully *obliterated* by the corruption of the Soul, and the ascendency that lust had gained'' (p. 6).

On account of the fall, by which the light of nature had become obscured, a written revelation through God's word was necessary. The Word, however, operates on men through their faculties—their wills, their consciences, their "passions," and their understandings. Hence reason, although impaired, is still in a position of high importance. "Thus," Colman declared, "God deals with us *as with rational Creatures,* and according to the nature and faculties he had given us: Wherein as he *puts honour* on Man's reason, so he shows how *great* a Sin it is in man to violate his own Reason and offend against it. We ought to *use* the reason GOD has given, yea and to *reverence* it: It is the rule and law of the Eternal and perfect *Infinite Mind* inscribed on us and *for* us: we shou'd reverence it as the *Wisdom of* GOD, as indeed it is'' (p. 8).

It will be noted that Colman did not recommend that reason be used in critical examination of theological doctrines. He himself never repudiated any of the traditional beliefs of the New England churches. What he represented was a change in manner or temper. As time passed, however, this mere reasonable manner was followed by a rationalistic examination of orthodox doctrines, which in many cases led to a repudiation of them.

Another minister who expressed a high appreciation of reason at this time was Experience Mayhew of Martha's Vineyard, who preached a sermon entitled *God Dealeth with Men as with Reasonable Creatures* in 1720. In support of his doctrine he presented two reasons. The first of these is that "GOD dealeth with Men as with Reasonable Creatures *because such they are, and it is very suitable that they should by* GOD *be dealt withal in such a Way as is agreeable to the Natures by Himself given unto them.''*

Since God created Nature and Man, in his government

of the world he makes use of the qualities with which he endowed created things. In his operations in the natural world he works "in, with, and by Second Causes, in a way agreeable to the Natural Qualities and Dispositions, which He Himself has put into them." In so doing, "God puts an Honour upon the works of His own Hands: He hereby shews that it is not in vain that He has put such Principles and Qualities into them, seeing He maketh use of them, and worketh with and by them in the government of the World" (p. 17).

"As therefore," Mayhew continued, "Inanimate and Irrational Creatures are governed in the way suitable to the Natures given unto them; so also Rationable and Intelligent Beings . . . are ruled and ordered in such a way, as is agreeable unto the excellent Natures with which they are indued. Man therefore being a Reasonable Creature, GOD constantly deals with him as such an One, treating him in a way agreeable to his Nature, and influencing of him by such Means as none but Intelligent Beings can be moved by."

Mayhew's second argument is that "GOD dealeth thus with Men, *Because the Nature of the Government which He has set up* over them *does* Necessarily call for it." "As GOD made Men capable of being governed by Laws with Sanctions, which Irrational Creatures are not; so he has determined to govern them by such Laws. . . . But now the Nature of this Kind of Government does require that Men be dealt with as Intelligent and Rational Beings, capable of acting as Free Agents; and of being influenced by Moral considerations, and if they were moved in any other way, as by meer Physical Influence, this would not agree unto the Nature of a moral subjection unto GOD, which consists in a Spontaneous, or Voluntary Obedience and Submission unto His Will: Therefore if men should in these things be dealt withal in any other way than as Reasonable Creatures, they could be no more said to obey GOD in their Motions, than Irrational Animals, and Creatures without Life, may be said to do'' (pp. 17-18).

A change of temper in New England at this time was manifested not only in a new emphasis on reason, but also in the development of what was known as a "catholick Spirit," or a tolerant recognition and understanding of differences in matters pertaining to religion. Of this, Colman was a conspicuous example. He himself, in a letter dealing with his sojourn in England, said of the development of this aspect of his nature "I did but grow in the *natural* Inclination I had to, and in the *generous* Principles of an enlarged *catholick* Spirit cherished in me by my *Tutor, Mr. Leverett*; now President of Harvard-College: And if I am able to judge, no Place of Education can well boast a more *free Air* than our little *College* may.'' [4]

The acceptance of the new science, the emphasis on reason, and the "catholick spirit" had not yet produced any actual doctrinal deviations from the traditional theology of New England. In 1726 Cotton Mather published a book entitled *Ratio Disciplinae Fratrum Nov-Anglorum,* which was almost wholly devoted to an explanation of the congregational church polity. In explaining why he did not deal with theology, he said: "There is no need of Reporting what is the *Faith* professed by the Churches in *New* England. For every one knows, That they perfectly adhere to the CONFESSION OF FAITH, published by the *Assembly* of Divines at *Westminster* . . ." "I cannot learn," he confidently declared, "That among all the Pastors of Two Hundred Churches, there is not *one* Arminian: much less an *Arian''* (p. 5).

Both Colman and Mayhew, as has been seen, had dealt with reason primarily as a human faculty to which God

---

[4] Ebenezer Turrell, *Life and Character of Dr. Benjamin Colman,* p. 123.

appeals in his dealings with mankind with reference to their beliefs and duties.

Meanwhile, a more positive view of reason, or the light of nature, as having an active role in the discovery of truth, had been expressed in a pamphlet written in connection with a controversy concerning church polity.

The distinguishing feature of the New England church polity was, as has been seen, the virtual autonomy of the individual congregations. These congregations elected their own ministers and otherwise conducted their own affairs without dictation from higher authority. It was provided, however, that, when a problem of doctrine or discipline arose in a congregation, a council composed of both clerical and lay delegates from neighboring churches could be called to deal with the situation. These councils could only rebuke and advise, however, and their decisions had no binding force. In the earlier period, when a high degree of unanimity prevailed, the decisions of councils had, nevertheless, been accepted as authoritative.

As divergencies and stresses appeared in the churches, however, some of the ministers felt a need for taking measures to maintain orthodoxy and uniformity. In 1705 these ministers held a meeting at which they drew up a set of *Proposals,* copies of which they dispatched to the other ministers of the colony. These *Proposals* recommended the introduction of authoritarian procedures and organizations which had hitherto been unknown. For instance, whereas formerly ministers had been elected by the congregations without the necessity of approval by higher authority, it was now proposed that a candidate for a pastorate be examined as to his fitness by the local ministerial association, which commonly included the ministers of a county. It was further recommended that the churches of an area, organized into a "consociation," should set up a regular and standing

47

council which would have authority to make binding decisions regarding church affairs within the area. This council would meet at stated times for deliberations. Thus the consociations of congregations and the ecclesiastical councils were to be permanent organizations endowed with authority, whereas in the past councils represented no fixed area—merely "neighboring churches"—and were called only when conditions in a congregation seemed to demand investigation and advice.

These *Proposals* were never put into effect in Massachusetts, although some of them were embodied in the Saybrook Platform in Connecticut, adopted in 1708.

To John Wise, of Ipswich, these *Proposals* seemed to be a threat to the liberties of the congregations which had been not only established by custom but also officially guaranteed by the *Cambridge Platform,* adopted by a synod in 1648, which was in effect a written ecclesiastical constitution.

To protect the liberties of the churches, Wise wrote two pamphlets: *The Churches Quarrel Espoused* (1713, 1715) and *A Vindication of the Government of the New England Churches* (1717). In supporting the constitution of the churches, Wise used three bases for his argument: Scripture, history, and reason.

Although the *Vindication* was written to meet a specific problem that confronted the New England Churches, Wise, in the section in which he employed reason as the basis for his argument, not only expressed a highly exalted view of the Light of Nature but also, on this basis, developed a general political philosophy of a highly democratic nature which was, he thought, applicable in both state and church.

Beginning with a declaration which related his defense of the New England church order to both his estimate of reason and his basic political philosophy, Wise said: "The Divine Establishment in Providence of the forenamed Churches in their Order is apparently the Royal assent of the supream Monarch of the Churches, to the grave decisions of Reason in favour of Man's Natural state of Being, and Original Freedom." "For if we should make a New *Survey* of the Constitution before named under the brightest Light of Nature, there is no greater Example of natural Wisdom in any settlement on Earth . . . than in this." Then, regarding the origin and basis of this constitution, he said: "That it seems to me as though Wise and Provident Nature by the Dictates of Right Reason excited by the moving suggestions of Humanity; and awed with the just demands of Natural Libertie, Equitie, Equality, and Principles of Self-Preservation, Originally drew up the Scheme and then obtained the Royal Approbation." Although this plan had actually been drawn up by men by the use of Right Reason, and had merely been approved by God, "it is agreeable that we attribute it to God whether we receive it nextly [directly] from Reason or Revelation." The reason for this is that each of these, reason and revelation, "is equally an Emanation of his Wisdom."

Then, expanding on the conception that reason is one of the two emanations of God's wisdom, Wise said: "The Spirit of Man is the Candle of the Lord, searching ·ll the inward parts of the Belly. There be many lar₀er Volumes in this dark Recess called the Belly to be read by that Candle God has Light up. And I am very well assured the fore named Constitution is a Transcript out of some of their Pages . . . *And the Life was the Light of Men, which Lighteth every Man which cometh into the World.* This admirable Effect of Christ's creating Power in hanging out so many Lights to guide man through a dark World, is as Applicable to the Light of Reason, as to that of Revelation." This is true because "the Light of Reason as a Law and Rule of Right, is an Effect of Christ's Goodness, care, and creating Power, as well as of Revelation.'' Wise added, however, that ''Revelation is Nature's Law in a fairer and brighter edition.''

Although Wise granted that revelation was a ''brighter and fairer edition'' of Nature's Law than reason provided, he did not give the usual explanation for this superiority. Unlike Colman, for example, he completely ignored the idea that man's reason had been seriously impaired as a result of the fall.

After thus showing how man, by means of reason or the light of nature, has a capacity for discovering truth, Wise undertook to ''disclose several Principles of Natural Knowledge; plainly discovering the Law of Nature; or the true sentiments of Natural Reason, with Respect to Man's Being and Government.'' These principles thus discovered by reason relate to man in two different states: (1) ''Natural,'' that is, as an individual not yet joined in a compact with others to form a civil society, and (2) ''the Civil Being of Man,'' that is, man as a member of an organized state. In this political section Wise said that he would take as his ''Chief Guide and Spokes-man'' Samuel Pufendorf, whose book had appeared in an English translation entitled *Of the Law of Nature and Nations* in 1710.

In considering man purely as an individual and without reference to any relations to society, Wise said that he would ''Explain the State of Humane Nature in its Original *Capacity,* as Man is placed on Earth by his Maker, and cloathed with many Investitures, and Immunities, which properly belong to Man separately considered.''

Wise then stated and discussed three ''immunities'' which are the privileges of man merely considered as a human being.

''The Prime Immunity in Man's State,'' he said, ''is that he is most properly the Subject of the Law of Na-

50

ture. He is the favourite Animal on Earth; in that this Part of God's Image, viz. Reason is congenite with his Nature, wherein by a Law Immutable, Instampt upon his Frame, God provided a Rule for Men in all their Actions. . . ."

"The Second Great Immunity of Man is," Wise said, "an Original Liberty Instampt upon his Rational Nature. He that intrudes upon this Liberty, violates the Law of Nature." Then, in a bold statement, Wise brushed aside one of the most cherished doctrines of the Calvinistic tradition of New England. "In this Discourse," he said, "I shall wave the consideration of Man's Moral Turpitude, but shall view him Physically as a Creature which God has furnished essentially with many Ennobling Immunities, which render him the most August Animal in the World, and still, whatever has happened since his Creation, he remains at the upper-end of Nature, and as such is a creature of a very Noble Character."

"The Third Capital Immunity belonging to Man's Nature, is," Wise said, "an equality amongst Men; which is not to be denied by the Law of Nature, 'till Man has Resigned himself with all his Rights for the sake of a Civil State . . ."

In considering man " in a civil state of being," Wise said: "Every man considered in a natural state, must be allowed to be free, and at his own dispose; yet to suit man's inclinations to society; and in a peculiar manner to gratify the necessity he is in of public rule and order, he is impelled to enter into a civil community; and divests himself of his natural freedom, and puts himself under government." "The formal reason of government is the will of a community, yielded up and surrendered to some other subject, either of one particular person, or more . . ." After discussing three forms of government in both state and church—monarchy, aristocracy, and democracy, Wise came to the following conclusion:

51

"It seems most agreeable with the light of nature, that if there be any of the regular government settled in the church of God it must needs be, a democracy. This is a form of government, which the light of nature does highly value, and often directs to as most agreeable to the just and natural prerogatives of human beings." With specific reference to the polity of the New England churches, which he considered to be democratic, he asserted, "This constitution is as agreeable with the light and laws of nature as any other whatsoever . . . and more accommodated to the concerns of religion than any other."

With reference to his specific purpose, the preservation of the constitution of the New England churches, Wise summarized his argument under "Three particulars; or so many golden maxims, securing the honor of congregational churches."

"Particular 1. That the people or fraternity [i.e., lay members of the church] . . . are the first subject of power; or else religion sinks the dignity of human nature into a baser capacity with relation to ecclesiastical, then it is in, in a natural state of being with relation to civil government.

Particular 2. That a democracy in church or state, is a very honorable and regular government to the dictates of right reason. And therefore,

Particular 3. That churches of *New-England,* in their ancient constitution of church order; it being a democracy, are manifestly justified and defended by the law and light of nature."

Wise's high estimate of the light of nature, or reason, and of political democracy were unique at the time. Presumably the persistence of the traditional doctrine of depravity precluded the general acceptance by Congregational ministers of such an exalted opinion of human nature, including human reason, as Wise put forth.

It was not long afterwards, however, that sermons on the relation between natural and revealed religion began to appear. In these sermons natural religion, based solely on the light of nature, is granted a genuine, though limited, validity.

In 1727, ten years after Wise's *Vindication,* Samuel Johnson, now an Anglican clergyman at Stratford, Connecticut, preached a sermon entitled *The Necessity of Revealed Religion.* Before treating his mean theme, Johnson said: "... it may be observed in the first place, that the light of nature has always discovered, that there is a glorious infinitely wise and powerful being, and that not only mankind, but all other beings are entirely dependent upon Him. The frame of the world, and the regularity, order and harmony of all the appearances in it, have always brought the whole race of mankind to this conclusion, so that there has scarce ever been found a society or community of men so far sunk below reason into sottishness and brutishness as to make any question of it" (III, 370).

Regarding the insufficiency of what was thus acquired, however, and hence the necessity of revelation, Johnson said: "Now whatever attainments in the true knowledge of God, any particular persons have advanced to, by the mere light of nature, who may have been extraordinary geniuses and had singular leisure and advantages for such speculations; yet it is certain that the generality of men have entertained but the darkest and grossest apprehensions of the Deity. So that the improvements of the natural light could never extend very far in the reforming of mankind, and begetting among them true apprehensions of God. And therefore a divine and supernatural revelation, if such could be had, would certainly be the most compendious and expeditious method of bringing mankind in general to a just sense of God."

"But," he added, "if we duly consider the general

53

state and condition of men, it will appear to be morally impossible for them to arrive at any tolerably right apprehensions of the divine nature without supernatural revelation" (III, pp. 272-273).

The next decade, 1730-1740, was a rather distinct period in New England religious history. In the year 1730, the centennial of the Massachusetts Bay Colony, several ministers took advantage of the occasion to deplore the decline in religious zeal and piety since the days of the founding fathers. Such lamentations were often accompanied by a plea for a revival of religion. In 1740 the revival, known as the Great Awakening, which constituted another epoch in New England religious history, began.

During the intervening decade the rationalistic spirit made further advances, and the status of the Calvinistic theology, which was rarely actually renounced, suffered considerably from dislike and neglect.

One of the retrospective centennial sermons of the year 1730 was *Observations Historical and Practical on the Rise and Primitive State of New England,* by Thomas Foxcroft. Most of the sermon gave an unfavorable comparison between the present generation and the colonists of 1630. The spirit of toleration which had developed was, to Foxcroft, not an unmixed blessing. After speaking of "the zeal for Reformation . . . which so distinguished our pious Ancestors," he asserted: "We pretend to excel them in a *Catholick Spirit,* as 'tis called, and to entertain more generous Principles than they; but alas have we not lost our Zeal for the great Substantials of Religion, as well as for peculiar Modalities: And is it not to be fear'd, that many under the glorious mask of Christian Charity hide a cold Indifference to all Religion" (p. 41).

Foxcroft was probably right in saying that the "Catholick Spirit" was sometimes a mask for religious indifference and it is certainly true that this spirit provided an atmosphere in which the rationalistic spirit could thrive, at least to a limited extent. Hence Foxcroft and other defenders of orthodoxy soon had reason to complain about the spread of a religion which they considered to be philosophical rather than Scriptural.

In the very year of Foxcroft's complaint, an extreme example of the rationalizing spirit appeared in an ordination sermon entitled *The Usefulness of Reveal'd Religion, to Preserve and Improve that which is Natural,* by John Bulkley.

"With Relation to the first *Thing, viz. Natural Religion,*" Bulkley said: "You may take this short Definition of it, viz. That it is that Faith and Observance or Obedience which Nature, or Natural Light teaches men." In words that suggest the point of view which Mather had presented in *The Christian Philosopher,* Bulkley continued: "By Nature here I would not be understood to intend simple, uninstructed Nature, but Nature or Natural light under its utmost improvement by Contemplation or Study of the works of God in Creation and Providence, those common discoveries he makes of himself and his will to all mankind" (p. 5).

"As for Reveal'd Religion," Bulkley said, "you may take this Account of it, viz., *That it is that Faith and Observance* which is taught in the *Scriptures or word of* God." Although Revelation is "superadded to the light of Nature," "Natural Religion" is actually the "Faith and Observance which is taught and recommended to us by this Divine, Supernatural Revelation!" Therefore, Bulkley declared, "Reveal'd Religion, or Christianity, as we commonly call it, is not a thing altogether different from Natural Religion, but contrarily . . . it is very much one, and the same thing, as I but now hinted: as to the main Part of it, no other than Natural Religion reinforced, and improved by Divine Revelation" (pp. 9-10).

Revealed religion does, however, include articles "which Nature makes no discovery of": the trinity, the origin of sin, the means of redemption, and "believing in Christ for Righteousness and Life."

Not only does revealed religion include items not found in natural religion, but it is also in "every way calculated, adapted or Suited to the preservation and furtherance of" natural religion. For this there are four reasons: (1) "it contains all the Truths of Natural Religion," (2) "it Illustrates, Explains, and Improves them," (3) "it corrects all the Errors and Corruptions that with or among any have crept into it," and (4) "it improves its Motives and adds to them" (p. 15).

Since natural religion is thus so much indebted to revealed religion, the "Word of God" is "Well deserving of our utmost Esteem, Affection and Regard." Since the Bible provides such a valuable service to natural religion, it is strange, Bulkley thought, "that the Deists of our age should seek to weaken its Authority, and procure its Banishment out of the world, by forming many senseless Objections, as they are wont to do." The Deists considered natural religion to be self-sufficient, and revelation to be unnecessary or impossible. Bulkley considered that, in view of the great service of revelation to natural religion, this position was inconsistent and insincere. "I must confess," he said, "I am at a loss to know what Religion (if any) such men would have. Natural Religion, rescued from its Errors and Corruptions, it's certain they would not; since were this (as some of them pretend) what they would, they would be more sparing in their Objections and Invectives against this Institution of Christians [the Bible], which has been shewed to be so proper a Mean to preserve and improve it. And it seems evident that either they would have no Religion at all (would burst all bonds and cast all cords from them) or some Religion opposite to the sincere and pure Dictates of Nature" (pp. 28-29).

Although Bulkley rebuked the Deists for their attitude toward revelation, he himself seemed to be most enthusiastic about the part of revealed religion that is identical with natural religion.

Bulkley recognized that his attitude was an unusual one, but was ready with a strong defense of it. Since the occasion of his sermon was the ordination of a young minister, other clergymen were present. Addressing himself to this part of the audience, he said: *"Reverend and much Esteemed,* I am sensible that in what I have said I have gone in a somewhat untrodden Path: and perhaps it may be tho't by some here present, that the Argument I have been upon is improper and very aliene from what might be expected on such an Occasion as this. However I can't think it altogether so, since as it's a matter well deserving to be more universally known and consider'd by Christians than it is, so furnishes me with fit matter of Address to you and me, and all others of our Character, one great Article of Duty, needful to be observed by us in the whole Course of our Ministry."

Then, advising the ministers, he declared this "great Article of Duty" to be: "That . . . we take care to shew due regard to the great, important matters of Natural Religion, and seek the furtherance of Persons in them by all the means we are capable of. For if the Preservation and Improvement of Natural Religion in the hearts and Lives of Men, be his great End therein, then this sure is what we also in the Course of our Ministry should very much scope at, and lay ourselves out in. 'Tis very obvious to everyone that reads the Scriptures, that the things falling under this Head, are there spoken of as of an Importance and Obligation above others: Those great Duties of Natural Religion, Judgment, Mercy and

Faith, are call'd *The weightier matters of the Law.* . . . And are all along spoken of as what GOD requires above, and are far more pleasing to him, than any things in Religion of a Ritual or positive Nature" (p. 34).

It is doubtful that Bulkley's recommendations had much direct effect on the preaching of the New England ministers. Nevertheless, the use of natural religion in sermons seems to have become common enough to alarm Thomas Foxcroft.

In 1732, two years after Bulkley's sermon, Foxcroft wrote a preface for a book entitled *The Reasonableness of Christianity,* a series of four sermons by Jonathan Dickinson. In addressing the reader, Foxcroft said: *"You will be asham'd* . . . of those *unevangelical* and (pretended) *rational* Christians, whether Preachers or Professors, whose favourite topick is the Religion of Nature, and whose darling Rules and Motives are of the Philosophic Kind . . . : who teach the Principles or practice the Duties of natural Religion, with little or no explicit Reference to a Redeemer, or Reduction of Things to a Gospel Model." The Gospel doctrines were, Foxcroft thought, "scandalously neglected, or indifferently regarded in the present day, by many Professors and Preachers even in the reforming World" (pp. x-xi).

Jonathan Dickinson, minister of a Presbyterian Church in Elizabeth-Town, New Jersey, was a native New Englander and a Yale graduate, who always kept in close touch with religious affairs in New England and with the New England ministers. In the book to which Foxcroft supplied the preface, he claimed that "The Being and Attributes of GOD, the Apostasy of Man, and the Credibility of the Christian Religion, are demonstrated by rational considerations . . . and vindicated against the most important Objections, whether of ancient or modern Infidels." Obviously Foxcroft thought that this was just the book New England needed at the moment.

Since Dickinson had promised to carry on his argument by rational considerations, he used the method of the physico-theology in the first sermon entitled "A demonstration of the Being and Attributes of God." Thereafter he argued mostly on a Scriptural basis.

In treating the Infidels, "whether ancient or modern," Dickinson placed his whole emphasis on their deficiencies. The positive merits of what could be learned by the light of nature he ignored completely.

To bring out the deficiencies of Deism, Dickinson exclaimed: "Here let the *Deist* try his skill: Let him without the assistance of *revelation,* draw up a perfect *system* of the laws of nature; let him consult the means of restoring our *lost innocency*; and of keeping our *affections* and *passions,* under the government of *religion* and *reason*: Let him call in the help of all the *Philosophers* of *Greece* and *Rome* for his assistance in this arduous undertaking: and in the conclusion, he'll have but his labour for his pains, and continue in the same inextricable *labyrinth.*"

"This," he continued, with reference to the philosophers of Greece and Rome, "is apparent from the fruitless pains of all the wisest *moral heathen* in this case; who, tho' all sensible of our *pravity* and misery, could never find out the *cause* nor *cure.* They have indeed, some of 'em, given excellent *moral rules,* for the government and conduct of human life. But then, these were all very defective in many essential *articles*; and their best *systems* have countenanc'd and encourag'd, even the grossest and most unnatural *impieties.*" "But," he asked, "what light have any, or all of 'em given, in the present enquiry? What *remedy* have any of their schools propos'd for our *misery?* What means to restore unto *reason* the empire of the mind, and to reduce the exorbitancy of the *passions* and appetites?'' (pp. 54-55).

Then, continuing his attack on the Deists in a sarcastic vein, Dickinson, searching for answers to the problems of life, asked: ''Shall we consult our *Oracles of Wit*, and seek some rational *scheme* of *religion* and happiness from our modern *pagans*, the *Deists*? These libertines can vainly boast of unprejudic'd *Reason* and *Science*, as tho' *they were the men, and wisdom must dy with them.* They can put out the *eyes* of *conscience*, and bravely scoff at reveal'd religion, as an idle dream, and the effect of a melancholy imagination, enthusiasm or *Priestcraft*. But which of 'em has ever pretended to propose a method of our obtaining inward *peace* and purity, *happiness* here, and *salvation* hereafter?'' (p. 61).

It should be noted that Foxcroft had in his preface dealt with the Religion of Nature as something that had too large a place in the preaching of some of the New England ministers. Dickinson, on the other hand, was attacking a more radical kind of religious thought which completely rejected revelation and which had actually flourished in England rather than in America. He, like other orthodox ministers, was afraid, however, that radical Deism would have an unfortunate effect in America.

None of the other published sermons of the decade positively supported the validity of the Light of Nature to the extent that Bulkley's had done. There is, however, a record of one instance of a view of the Light of Nature more extreme than Bulkley's. In 1733, the next year after Foxcroft's complaint about ministers who preached in a too philosophical vein, Robert Breck, after graduating from Harvard in 1730, was preaching temporarily in Windham, Connecticut. There, as was reported later, he made statements about the Light of Nature in his sermons which were soon to be a source of trouble for him. In 1734, Breck was elected minister of a church in Springfield. Before he was ordained, however, unfavorable reports about his doctrine reached Springfield and the ministers of the Hampshire County ministerial association attempted to prevent his ordination. For this purpose they assembled testimony from people who had known of Breck's preaching in Connecticut. Among those who sent in letters about him was Thomas Clap, later to be Rector of Yale. In the part of the letter pertaining to doctrine, Clap said, "He preached, *That the Heathen that liv'd up to the Light of Nature should be Saved, & Christ should be immediately Revealed to them or they should be Saved in some other way, and that the contrary was a harsh Doctrine.*" It was also reported that in conversation about the point Breck had said that "he would beat the People out of those false and stingy Notions which they had been taught." Six other letters from Connecticut gave similar testimony.

In spite of the strenuous efforts of the ministers of the county association, a majority of the members of the Springfield congregation stood by their choice and Breck was ordained. During the ceremony, however, in order to satisfy his critics, he presented a "confession of faith" in which he not only stated the main points of New England orthodoxy but also repudiated the point which had been the main cause of opposition to him. "I believe," he said, "that *there is a God,* whose eternal Power and Godhead are to be clearly seen from the Things which he has made: But I believe the Light of Nature is no way sufficient to lead us into the true Knowledge of what God is, and what he requires of us, in order to our Glorifying him here, and coming to the Enjoyment of him hereafter."

It was not only Congregational clergymen who were at this time concerned about the spread of natural religion and Deism. The Anglican Samuel Johnson had observed the development of Deism in England, which,

61

he thought, was the result of too much reliance on reason to the exclusion of faith. In explanation of this view he said, writing of himself in the third person: "What the more confirmed him in these conclusions was that he observed in the course of his time, that Arianism and Latitudinarianism so much in vogue often issued in Socinianism and that in Deism and that in atheism and the most dissolute living; that the more gentlemen pretended to reason and deep speculation the more they dwindled in faith and the more they pretended to demonstrate what they called natural religion and morality, the more irreligious and immoral they grew, and that in proportion as they grew more conceited and self-sufficient." It was, he said, "melancholy to observe the gradual but deplorable progress of infidelity and apostacy in this age of mighty pretense and reasoning from the well meaning but too conceited Mr. Locke, down to Tindal, and thence to Bolingbroke, etc. etc." (I, 23).

After further sketching the growth of Deism in England and the controversies about it, Johnson said, "And soon after this . . . Tindal comes out with a plausible piece called *Christianity as Old as the Creation*, built upon some unguarded expressions of some of our best divines, seeming to admit that the great principles of natural religion and morality were clearly known by the light of nature, whence he argued against any necessity of revelation." After an account of Deistic works that followed Tindal's book and of replies to them, Johnson observed: "It was a pity our divines had not been more careful to define natural religion to mean (as it truly does) that part of religion which is founded in the nature of God and man and the relation we stand in to Him, and one another and not to imply that even that part of religion would ever have been discovered by the mere light of nature uninstructed, especially in the present condition of human nature, as is abundantly evident from universal fact" (I, 23-24).

As has been seen. Johnson had experienced a sense of relief when, in 1714-1715, he had been converted from the old learning to the new philosophy and science. In his present situation he found help in the idealistic philosophy of George Berkeley. In February, 1729, Berkeley had arrived at Newport, Rhode Island, where he lived for over two years. While he was there Johnson visited him and he also carried on a correspondence on philosophical topics with him in 1729-30.

Regarding the result of this association with Berkeley, Johnson said: "This was of vast use to Mr. Johnson and cleared up many difficulties in his mind, both philosophical and theological, as he found the Dean's way of thinking and explaining things, utterly precluded scepticism and left no room for endless doubts and uncertainties. His denying matter at first seemed shocking, but it was only for want of giving a thorough attention to his meaning." Johnson had been afraid that Berkeley's philosophy was inconsistent with Newtonianism, but after Berkeley had assured him that the laws of physics were not invalidated by the fact that matter exists only as ideas, he was satisfied. He also decided that the idealistic philosophy was attended with "this vast advantage, that it not only gave new incontestible proofs of a deity, but moreover, the most striking apprehensions of his constant presence with us and inspection over us, and of our entire dependence on him and infinite obligations to his most wise and almighty benevolence" (I, 25).

The growth of the rationalistic spirit did not, as some of the ministers feared, lead to the acceptance of Deism or of Natural Religion to the exclusion of Christianity in New England. It did, however, weaken the position of the Calvinistic doctrines. For this reason some of the conservative ministers were alarmed about the spread of Arminianism.

The first and most vigorous of these complaints about Arminianism was contained in *New-England's Lamentations,* by John White, of Gloucester, published in 1734, only eight years after Cotton Mather had asserted that there was not a single Arminian among the ministers of the New England churches.

"It is a Matter of Lamentation," White declared, that some of the young ministers "are under *Prejudice against,* and fall off from, important Articles of the *Faith* of these *Churches,* and cast a favourable Eye upon, embrace, and as far as they dare, *argue* for, *propagate* and *preach* the *Arminian Scheme.*" White gave as a cause of the spread of Arminianism the reading of modern books. "Our young Men," he said, "are apt to look upon old Books, as Men do upon old Houses, to be of little Worth; because not built to the new Mode." They hear of these books from those who have been corrupted by them, "and these corrupt Books being very agreeable to a nice Taste, as to their Language, and as agreeable to the Matter, suiting their Proud and self conceited Hearts, by extolling *free Will* and *self Sufficiency*: They presently and greedily suck in those Opinions." Being thus misled, these young men "never peruse our *professed Principles* impartially and without Prejudice, and are ready to reject them before they understand them." Hence "these accursed, poisonous and Soul damning Principles, being wrap'd up in sweet *Language,* are swallowed down and retained" (p. 26).

During this time Jonathan Edwards did not comment directly on the state of religion in New England. It seems probable, however, that he had been observing the tendency to attribute more and more efficacy to man's own efforts in the process of regeneration. He himself was devoted to the old Calvinistic doctrine of the absolute sovereignty of God not only intellectually but emotionally, and he therefore minimized the independence of man and his efforts. This point of view he expressed in his first published sermon, entitled *God Glorified in the Work of Redemption by the Greatness of Man's Dependence upon Him in the Whole of It,* delivered in 1731. In this sermon Edwards not only reasserted the old doctrine of God's sovereignty and man's dependence but also introduced some original speculation about the nature of the good enjoyed by the regenerate. "The redeemed," he said, "have all their good *in God.*" This good is of two kinds—"objective or inherent." The objective good is that "extrinsic object, in the possession and enjoyment of which they are happy." "He is the highest good . . . The glorious excellencies and beauty of God will be what will for ever entertain the minds of the saints . . .".

While the "objective good" is outside of man, the "inherent good is that excellency or pleasure which is in the soul itself." This "inherent good is two-fold; it is either excellency or pleasure." The regenerate have "spiritual excellency and joy by a kind of participation of God." Regarding the first aspect of the "inherent good," Edwards said that the redeemed "are made excellent by a communication of God's excellency. God puts his own beauty . . . upon their souls." As to the second aspect of this good, Edwards said that "The saint hath spiritual joy and pleasure by a kind of effusion of God on the soul" just as "the moon and planets are bright by the sun's light."[5]

The dependence of man on God in the process of regeneration was presented in a different manner by Edwards three years later in a sermon entitled *A Divine and Supernatural Light Immediately Imparted to the Soul by the Spirit of God* (1734). Other divines had

---

[5] Faust and Johnson, *op. cit.,* pp. 98-99.

recently been concerned about the necessity of revelation for supplying religious truths which could not be ascertained by the light of nature. They were therefore concerned mainly about matters of belief or doctrine with reference to salvation. Edwards, on the other hand, was particularly concerned with what takes place in the soul in the process of regeneration.

Edwards admittted that "natural conscience or reason will, by mere nature, make a man sensible of guilt, and will accuse and condemn him when he has done amiss." Also God may work on these natural abilities to heighten the feeling of guilt even in unregenerate men. "But," he said, "in the renewing and sanctifying work of the Holy Ghost, those things are wrought in the soul that are above nature, and of which there is nothing of the like kind in the soul by nature."

In explaining the nature of the change wrought in the soul by regeneration, Edwards made use of philosophical conceptions of the mind. In the work of regeneration, he thought, a spiritual and divine light is imparted to the soul. As a result of this, the regenerated man has "A true sense of the divine and superlative excellency of the things of religion." For instance, "He does not merely believe that God is glorious, but he has a sense of the gloriousness of God in his heart."

Then, giving the philosophical basis for the distinction between belief and "sense," Edwards said: "There is a twofold understanding or knowledge of good that God has made the mind of man capable of. The first, that which is merely speculative and notional; as when a person only speculatively judges that any thing is, which by the agreement of mankind, is called good or excellent . . . And the other is, that which consists in a sense of the heart: as when there is a sense of the beauty, amiableness, or sweetness of a thing; so that the heart is sensible of pleasure and delight in the presence of the idea of it. In the former is exercised merely the speculative faculty, or the understanding, strictly so called... In the latter, the will, or inclination of the heart."[6]

To Edwards, then, the distinguishing feature of regeneration was the imparting to the soul a light which produced a proper sense of divine things. In this process it is the will more than the understanding that is involved. This attitude, much elaborated, was later to be basic in some of Edwards' most important works.

Although Edwards was, in these sermons, reasserting the old conception of God's sovereignty, he used, in so doing, philosophical ideas concerning the good and the human mind that are not found in the writings of either his predecessors or his contemporaries. The use of novel philosophical material to protect old theological doctrines continued to be a characteristic of Edwards' work in later years when new situations were to be met.

Although Edwards was chiefly concerned with the relative importance of the understanding and the will, other ministers were more likely to occupy themselves with the relations between natural and revealed religion or between reason and revelation. Two years after Edwards' sermon on *A Divine and Supernatural Light*, Jared Eliot dealt fully with this latter theme in a sermon entitled *The Two Witnesses* (1736) in which he demonstrated *"The great Usefulness both of Reason and of Divine Revelation in Religion."*

In defense of reason, Eliot said: "Some have thought it their duty, to depreciate and undervalue *Reason,* as not to be consider'd in Religion; have represented it as useless and dangerous. That they might do the greater Honour to Divine Revelation, by a voluntary Humility, have discarded it from any concern in Religion, and have thought themselves the better Christians for doing so. Whereas it is a strong Evidence for Religion and one of

6 Faust and Johnson, *op. cit.,* pp. 106-107.

its great Supports. It is disgraced with the opprobrious Names of *Carnal Reason,* and *Blind Reason.*" Eliot declared that if by "carnal reason," the detractors mean mere "confident Sophistry . . . called Demonstration," they were talking about "not *Reason,* but . . . only its Shadow." "But," he said, "if they mean *Reason it self* that they would condemn, they undervalue the most noble Faculty of our Soul, slay one of the Witnesses, promote *Enthusiasm,* and deprive Religion of one grand Support" (p. 64).

Men make a mistake also, "If on the other hand," they "overvalue their *Reason,* lay too great a stress upon it; and despise or deny all that will not come within the compass of it." "This over-valuing of Reason," Eliot said, "tends to promote Atheism, Deism and every Kind of Infidelity. As *Reason* is the distinguishing Character of man, so men are vain and conceited, and think themselves to be much wiser than they are; and while they would shew themselves wise, they discover themselves to be fools." "We should," he declared, "have a just Value for *Reason* and *Revelation.* Let not these which God has joined together, be by any man under any pretence put asunder" (p. 65).

Eliot demonstrated the folly of the Deist, who, relying solely on reason or the light of nature and neglecting revelation, fails to acquire complete and satisfying doctrines. Of such a Deist, he said: "If he be true to his Principles, he believes that there is a GOD, Holy and Just; therefore hates Sin and will punish it. He believes GOD is good; but this gives him no assurance that God will Pardon his Sins, though he repent of it. We can know nothing by the light of Nature but this, That a merciful and good GOD will Pardon, if it be wise and just that he should do so: . . . but whether it be so or no; he that owns no Revelation cannot tell. . . . But by Divine Revelation, we find that upon Repentance, we shall obtain Pardon'' (p. 65).

A less sanguine estimate of reason was given by Samuel Phillips in *The Orthodox Christian,* a book for children published in 1738. Although Phillips did not deal with the positive value of reason as Eliot had done, he agreed with him about its misuse by the Deists. "I am sensible," he said, "there are some called *Deists* who cast Contempt upon Revelation, crying up the *Perfection of Reason,* and of natural Light; now, although I freely acknowledge, that Reason, abstractedly considered, is not imperfect, (for Truth, doubtless is Truth, and right Reason is right Reason) yet I deny the perfection of Reason, as it is *now* in Men; *viz.* in their State of Degeneration; Or, that it is sufficient to discover them; all that they are to believe concerning *God,* and all the Methods necessary for them to take in order to be reconciled to Him, and regain his Favour; or, indeed, *all* that is requir'd of them in their several Relations, and in their various conditions in Life" (p. ii).

These defects are found not only in the modern Deists but also in the ancient pagan thinkers. In their works, Phillips said, "we may easily discern the insufficiency of Natural Light, and the necessity of Revelation" (p. ii).

In the course of the decade a combination of religious indifference and the rationalistic spirit had produced changes which were deplored by ministers who were faithful to the traditional theology of New England.

One of these ministers was William Cooper of the Brattle Street Church in Boston. To counteract the doctrinal laxity of the time, Cooper wrote a book entitled *The Doctrine of Predestination unto Life,* published in the spring of 1740. Although the doctrines of the New England churches were essentially Calvinistic in nature, the New England divines had not been in the habit of using the Calvinistic label. Now that these doctrines seemed to be jeopardized, the name was adopted, apparently to clarify the issue. This step was taken by five ministers of Boston who, in a preface to Cooper's book, declared that they were Predestinarians and Calvinists and that the doctrine of predestination was one of the essential doctrines of the Reformation. Cooper himself, to show why an explanation and defense of the doctrine was now needed, said that although the doctrine was "illustrious and very precious," "Yet 'tis not only deny'd by many, but decried and reproach'd by many as unworthy of God, and prejudicial to religion; while others who don't care to deny it, yet speak of it as amongst those mysterious, controversial, and speculative points, which it is best not to meddle with; and so they would have it smother'd in the Church, and shut out of our sermons" (p. 5).

A few years later, during the Great Awakening, two retrospective accounts of the changes which had taken place during the preceding years were published. One of these, published in *The American Magazine and Historical Chronicle* in September, 1743, was included in an article entitled "A Dissertation on the State of Religion in North America." Although this article was devoted mainly to the current revival, the writer gave some attention to the changes in preaching that had taken place just before it began. From the first settlement until recently, the writer said, the ministers had in their sermons stressed the "Doctrine of Regeneration, with those Convictions and Distresses looked upon as inseparable concomitants" and to such doctrines as "Original Sin, Justification by Faith alone, &c." "The precepts of Morality," he said, "had not been so much attended to . . ." Then "a few years before these Commotions began . . . some of the Clergy began to preach less metaphysical and more practical Sermons; on which many

70

People complain'd of the Decay of Religion, the Absence of that fervour and Spirituality that had formerly appeared among Ministers and People, and the danger of Arminianism overspreading the Land" (pp. 1-2).

The influence of the rationalistic spirit among the people in general in the years just before the revival was described in a pamphlet entitled *The Testimony and Advice of a Number of Laymen Respecting Religion, and the Teachers of It,* dated September 12, 1743. This *Testimony* was "Addres'd to the Pastors of New England," and was mainly a rebuke to the ministers who, as these laymen thought, constituted a party which supported George Whitefield for their own advantage. In explaining the genesis of this party, the laymen gave an account of the situation preceding the revival as it was viewed by some of the ministers. "Now," they said, "the Leaders of the *Party-zealot Pastors* (who were rigid favourers of the Doctrines of *Calvinism* . . .) having observed for some years past, that Freedom of Inquiry had very much prevail'd among the people, more especially among the Students at the Colleges; and that of late years many had us'd in themselves to examine with Candor what Evidence any Opinion or Principle had to support and prove its Truth, that they rejected and exploded all Opinions and Doctrines that were themselves absurd or that had but weak and lame Proofs to maintain them; and that by means of certain valuable Books wrote by some of the ablest and best men in the Nation [i.e., England], Bigotry, Superstition, and an implicit Faith to what the Clergy said were considerably worn off, and were every Day more and more dying away; and knowing that as much as Bigotry, Superstition, &c wore off, and Freedom of Inquiry for the Proof of Doctrines advanc'd and taught, took Place and increas'd, by so much must their Influence and the Calvinistical Principles . . . subside and die away, . . . they thought the

71

most likely and probable Way to promote and revive
their Party, and their religious Tenets, (which at this
Time were at very low ebb) and to set themselves at the
Head both of Pastors and People, was to secure and
bring Him [Whitefield] over to their Interest" (p. 5).

II

THE GREAT AWAKENING: 1740-1745

During the period of the growth of rationalism and
the "decay of vital religion" there had been many calls
for a revival. And there had, in fact, been several local
and temporary revivals. The general and prolonged religious awakening, which the local ministers had not been
able to effect, was initiated by two outsiders: George
Whitefield, a clergyman of the Church of England, and
Gilbert Tennent, a Presbyterian of New Jersey.

With the coming of the revival, the religious conditions
of New England were changed abruptly and radically.
While a leading characteristic of the preceding period
had been the growth of the rationalistic spirit, a domi-
nant feature of the revival was the prevalence of emotionalism. This created an occasion for controversy about
the relative roles of both the emotions and reason in
religion.

The emotionalism of the revival, like other features of
it to which critics objected, was largely due to the example of George Whitefield, who, before coming to New
England, had already, along with his friends John and
Charles Wesley, initiated a revival in England. In England even more than in New England the first part of
the eighteenth century had been characterized by luke-
warmness in religion and by rationalism which culmi-

nated in Deism. Against this condition the revival headed by Whitefield and the Wesleys was a protest.

Whitefield was by natural gifts and experience perfectly fitted for the role he assumed. Deeply emotional, he had experienced extreme spiritual dejection at times before his conversion and intense elation immediately afterwards. This conversion had been experienced suddenly in the solitude of his Oxford room. When Whitefield began to preach soon afterwards, his main theme was the necessity of the New Birth, a sudden and palpable change such as his own had been. This sudden change was attested by the Witness of the Spirit, or an inner feeling of certitude. This idea of an instantaneous New Birth was in sharp contrast with the prevailing Anglican conception of regeneration as a gradual process beginning with baptism and continuing imperceptibly throughout life and also contingent on good works. Whitefield's conviction of the necessity of the New Birth rested on his conviction of man's depravity and this constituted his only theological equipment at the beginning of his preaching career. To this, however, he soon added the other Calvinistic points. In theology, therefore, he differed sharply from the great body of the Anglican clergy, who were Arminian. To Whitefield it seemed that doctrinally they had sunk into a kind of "refined Deism."

For impressing on audiences his ideas about depravity, which he expressed by describing man as "half beast and half devil," and about the necessity of the New Birth, Whitefield was ideally equipped. Gifted with a powerful voice with a wide range of expressiveness and with other histrionic abilities, he could reach huge crowds and arouse in them both terror and joy.

Whitefield was also prone to believe that dreams can forecast actual events. Of this he recorded three instances which occurred not far from the time of his conversion. He also believed that in undertaking religious missions and in the preaching of sermons he received direct guidance and assistance from the Holy Spirit.

Not only did Whitefield denounce the English clergy but he was himself denounced by them. On account of his ideas and conduct he was labeled an enthusiast and was excluded from most of the Church of England pulpits. As a result he became an itinerant evangelist, usually preaching in the fields.

After thus preaching in England and the southern and middle colonies of America, Whitefield came to New England on the invitation of Benjamin Colman and William Cooper. In arousing religious zeal and reasserting Calvinistic doctrines, he was the answer to their frequently expressed prayers. This revival, however, produced problems which had not been anticipated by those who had asked for it, and it was therefore attended with fierce and voluminous controversy.

Whitefield arrived in Boston on September 18, 1740. There the reaction to his preaching was both favorable and unfavorable. Thomas Prince, in reporting on his sermon at the Old South Church, said: "He spake with a mighty sense of God, Eternity, the Immortality and Preciousness of the Souls of the Hearers, of their original Corruption, and of the extream Danger the unregenerate are in; with the Nature and absolute Necessity of Regeneration by the *Holy Ghost*; and of believing in CHRIST, in order to our Pardon and Justification. . . . His Doctrine was plainly that of the *Reformers*: Declaring against putting our *good Works* or *Morality* in the Room of *Christ's* Righteousness, or their having any Hand in our Justification, or being indeed pleasing to God while we are totally unsanctified, acting from corrupt Principles, and unreconciled Enemies to him." This, Prince said, "occasion'd some to mistake him as if he oppos'd *Morality*." He admitted that Whitefield "now

74

and then dropped some Expressions that were not so accurate and guarded as we should expect from aged and long studied Ministers."[1]

Thomas Foxcroft, who had been alarmed by the spread of the rationalistic spirit, was naturally delighted to have this trend counteracted by the preaching of Whitefield. On October 23, 1740, after Whitefield had been in New England a little over a month, Foxcroft delivered a sermon entitled *Some Seasonable Thoughts on Evangelic Preaching,* in which he not only extolled Whitefield but also again rebuked ministers whose sermons were too exclusively moralistic and philosophical.

Regarding the change that had taken place since Whitefield's arrival, Foxcroft said, "And here I wou'd take a publick Notice of it with Thankfulness to God, that a Spirit of *Zeal to the House of God* is awakened in many at this Day" (p. 22).

Most of the sermon is devoted to the theme that it is the duty of ministers to preach real Christian doctrine instead of mere moral and philosophical sermons. "With what Face," he said, "can we call ourselves *Christian* Ministers, if our preaching is upon the Principles and Laws of *Nature* (tho' taken into Christianity) while we consider 'em only under their *natural* Form, under the notion of meer *Morality,* or *Natural Religion*; forgetting that by their being incorporated into the *Gospel,* they have lost *that* Respect, chang'd their *Use* and End, put on a *new* Form, and in Effect are turn'd into *Evangelic* Principles and Rules, so that there's (strictly speaking) nothing at all meerly *moral,* nothing purely *natural* in the Christian *Creed* or *Canon.*" "Sure I am," he continued, "that to *philosophise* merely, without an Eye to Revelation, or to harangue upon *natural* Truths and *moral* Duties, in a rational Way, without reducing them to their proper Place and Use in the *Christian* Scheme,

---

[1] *Christian History,* ed. Thomas Prince (Boston, 1743-1745) II, 380.

... this is not ... to *preach the Kingdom of God.* What tho' the *Text* be taken out of the *Bible!* If the Sermon be in a philosophical and unevangelic Strain, the Preacher might as well have taken his Text out of *Seneca's* Morals" (p. 29). In a footnote to the published sermon, Foxcroft added, "I think, I cou'd readily direct an Inquirer where he may find many *Sermons,* that run to a faulty Excess upon a *philosophic Strain.*" As examples he cited two sermons by Tillotson (p. 33).

In contrast with this philosophical religion Foxcroft expounded what he took to be the evangelical principles as stated by St. Paul. "And," he said, with reference to Whitefield, "I can't forbear observing here, We have in a fresh Instance seen this *Pauline* Spirit and Doctrine remarkably exemplify'd among us. We have seen *a Preacher of Righteousness, fervent in Spirit,* teaching *diligently the Things of the Lord.*" Then, speaking for the clergy, he declared, "And as for *us,* we have been surpriz'd. We have been pleas'd. And shall we not now strive to imitate" (p. 43).

Although Whitefield found religious conditions in New England better than in England, he still found cause for complaint. Most of the ministers, he feared, "did not experimentally know Christ." The light of Harvard and Yale had become darkness. The New England colleges had sunk almost as low as the English universities as far as religion was concerned. He was particularly displeased with Harvard where the students read "bad books." Instead of the old evangelical writers, they read John Tillotson and Samuel Clarke, both of whom represented the kind of merely moral and philosophical religious thinking which excluded essential Christian doctrines.

After leaving New England on October 29, Whitefield arranged for the revival to be carried on by Gilbert Tennent, who belonged to the evangelical wing of the Presbyterians of New Jersey and whose doctrines and manner

76

of preaching were much like Whitefield's own. Tennent preached in New England for about two months in the winter of 1740-41.

"And shall we not now strive to imitate," Foxcroft had said to the ministers in commending the work of Whitefield. The sentiment was obviously held by many. After the departure of Whitefield and Tennent, the revival was carried on by native New Englanders until Whitefield returned in 1744. Some of the ministers conducted revivalistic meetings in their own parishes and others, like Whitefield, became itinerants. Furthermore, many uneducated laymen, known as "exhorters," turned to itinerant preaching. It was these who were responsible for many of the disorders of which even promoters of the revival complained.

Controversy about the revival began even while Whitefield and Tennent were in New England and from this time until September, 1745, almost all the significant religious publications were devoted wholly or in part to the revival.

Broadly speaking, both the clergy and laymen of New England were, in their attitude toward the revival, divided into two classes: "opposers" and supporters or promoters. There were, however, relatively few who accepted all aspects of it as good or, on the other hand, condemned it all as bad. The most common attitude was acknowledgment of a revival which was the work of God but which was marred by an admixture of errors and imprudences along with genuine religion. Among those who held this view there were some who gave most weight to the excesses, while others saw a balance in favor of the benefits of the revival.

The kind of revivalism which gave grounds for the attitude of the "opposers" was vividly described in a communication describing "the religious Commotions in the Colony of Connecticut" published in *The Boston*

Post-Boy of September 28, 1741, after the revival had
been in progress one year. "In general," the writer said,
"things appear in two very different and contrary Aspects, and Men are greatly divided in their Opinion,
according as they happen most Intensely to view the one
or the other." "On the one side," he acknowledged,
"these religious Commotions have produced a general
Concern upon the Minds of Men, a Reformation from
some Vices and Follies, and some seem to have passed
thro' a saving Change; and so far all good Men rejoice."

After this brief acknowledgment of the benefits of the
revival, the writer gave a longer and more spirited account of the undesirable aspects. Regarding the itinerants and their preaching, he said: "Some Ministers pretend to immediate Impression from the Spirit to leave
their own People a long time, and to travel about Preaching every Day in the Week, and by vertue of such Commission, they suppose they have sufficient Warrant to
go into other Men's Pulpits, or at least into their special charge, without their desire or consent; and they
have laid aside their Studies, Notes & Preparations, upon
pretence of being immediately impressed by the Spirit
what to Preach, and some of them have declared that
almost all they Preach is by the immediate Impressions
of the Holy Ghost putting a long Chain of Thoughts into
their Minds and Words into their Mouths. And their
main Design in Preaching seems not so much to inform
Men's Judgments as to terrify and affright their Imaginations, and by awful Words and frightful Representations, to set the Congregation into hideous Shrieks and
Out-cries." Giving further details of the effects of such
preaching, the writer said: "Some will faint away, fall
down upon the Floor, wallow and foam; some Women
will rend off their Caps, Handkerchiefs and other
Cloaths, tear their Hair down about their Ears, and
seem perfectly bereav'd of their Reasons."

Regarding the after-effects of such experiences the writer said: "After a little while, commonly next Day, some will come perfectly to their Right Mind, and have no Remembrance of what is past: But some are suddenly fil'd with Exstasies, Raptures and Transports of Joy, and an infallible Assurance: And generally with a bitter, censorious and uncharitable Spirit against all such as have not experienced these Raptures, or that don't look upon them as evidence of an extraordinary and miraculous Conversion. When they are once thus enlightened, they pretend to a Spirit of discerning, and by comparing Experiences, can tell who are converted, and who are not, with so much Certainty as that they cannot be deceiv'd in one Instance in a Hundred."

This account covered features of the revival which were criticized in scores of sermons, controversial pamphlets, books, and newspaper articles written by both opponents and moderate supporters.

The intrusion of itinerants into parishes where they had not been invited was thought to be destructive of the established order of the Congregational Churches. Following supposed impulses from the Holy Spirit in undertaking preaching tours and reliance on inspiration for the substance of sermons were taken to be "enthusiasm." Preaching without previous study or preparation was thought to show a contempt for learning which would eventually make the colleges seem unnecessary. The physical and emotional agitation induced by the revivalists were judged to be mere disorder, with no religious significance. Reliance on an intense emotional experience rather than on reformation of conduct as evidence of conversion was said to lead to Antinomianism. To some critics all such supposed conversions seemed spurious. The idea that conversion was an instantaneous experience of which the exact time could be known was taken to be an erroneous doctrine. Likewise the idea

79

that one could have assurance of conversion was considered a false doctrine. People who thought that emotional and instantaneous conversion was the only genuine kind and that after such conversion they had the gift of discerning whether others were converted were accused of unchristian censoriousness.

Another characteristic of the revivalists, implied but not stated in the above account, was, as John Caldwell of New Londonderry, New Hampshire, said: "They lay aside *Reason,* the *Candle* of the Lord. They will not be dealt with in that Way, nor regard its Dictates, they are unreasonable Men, from whom we ought all to pray . . . that we may be delivered."

Not only did the revivalists "lay aside *Reason,*" but some of them actually attacked it as dangerous. Since such attacks do not appear in any of the publications of the time, they were probably made in the extemporaneous sermons of itinerant ministers and exhorters. The rationalistic spirit which had been developing before the Awakening, however, was not completely quenched by the current wave of enthusiasm. This rationalistic attitude is not only implicit in many of the criticisms of the revival but was very explicitly expressed in some defenses of reason published in Boston newspapers in 1742.

A contributor to *The Boston Evening-Post* of January 4, 1742, observed: "Some Preachers of late having declared themselves mortal Foes to *Humane Reason,* in Matters of Religion, as a thing dangerous and destructive to the Souls of Men, and are heard snarling at REASON (that fair offspring of the Father of Light) in a most rude and opprobrious Manner, that one may well INFER, that they have *no Part or Lot in that Matter.*" He declared, however, that the Hebrew prophets and the apostles had been supporters of reason and also that "the most eminent Divines of our Nation [England] for learning and Holiness have labour'd more abundantly

in the Rational Way of Preaching." Then in defense of
reason he quoted at length from *A Learned and Elegant
Discourse on the Light of Nature* by Nathanael Culver-
wel, a Cambridge Platonist. The text used for this discourse was "The understanding of man is the candle
of the Lord."

Shortly after this Andrew Croswell, of Groton, Connecticut, was in the Boston area on a preaching tour.
While there he publicly stated that most of the ministers
and people of Boston were unconverted and also held
erroneous doctrines. Someone who had heard about
Croswell's remarks published a protest in *The Boston
Weekly News-Letter* of April 9, 1742. Advising Croswell
on how to deal with people suspected of error, he said:
"To be sure you should treat them as *reasonable* Creatures. . . . You ought to endeavour to convince their
Judgments, as well as move their Passions, for *without
Knowledge* the *Mind cannot be good*." Anticipating what
Croswell's reaction to his appeal might be, he inserted
a defense of reason. "But," he said, "now that I have
mentioned *Reason* and *Knowledge* I expect I shall be
judged a *carnal Socinian,* or *Arminian*. . . . However,
this I know, that the *Understanding* of Man is the *Candle
of the Lord*; and tho' Adam's Candle aspiring to be a
Sun has burnt the dimmer ever since, yet it is a great
and Royal Gift of our Creator; so that to blaspheme
Reason is to reproach Heaven itself, and to dishonour
the God of Reason, who has given it to us as a *handmaid
to Faith,* which is never *contrary to right Reason*."

Later in the spring, *The Boston Evening-Post* of June
7 carried a contribution entitled "A Modest *Proposal
for the Destruction of Reason*," an ironical defense of
reason written in the manner of Jonathan Swift.

"The Disadvantages Mankind lye under from the Exercise of *reason,* are so many and great," the writer
said, "that I wonder it has not been extirpated from the

Earth long ago. It is commonly called a *noble Faculty,* but whether it be so or not, this I am sure of, that it has a Faculty of doing an infinite deal of Mischief; what Confusion and Bloodshed has it occasioned? Witness the Establishment of the *Reformation*; and the Revolution of 1688.'' ''I shall therefore endeavour particularly,'' he promised, ''to point out the *Evils* arising from the free Use of it, and then propose some infallible *Methods* of destroying it.'' Obviously referring to the preaching of some of the revivalistic preachers, the writer said, ''And as I am now joining Heart and Hand with several Genius's that have lately shone in *these Parts,* I doubt not of Success, especially as this Monster has not committed such Ravages in this climate as in some others.''

Reason had had bad effects in four ways.

First the writer discussed briefly the bad effects in the political realm, of which the Revolution of 1688 was an example.

To religion he gave more attention. ''Another bad Effect of REASON,'' he said, ''is a Right that many (I can't say, *most* Men) assume in judging of Matters of Religion. This is much more intolerable than the other, as the Thing itself is of greater Importance; and should this Impudence prevail among us, it is to be feared, that those worthy Gentlemen, who are now promoting the Good of this people by decrying REASON; and abound in their Labours for that End ... will be defeated in their glorious Designs; and what the fatal Consequence of that will be, is easy to foresee.'

The other two points refer to more specific matters connected with religion.

The first of these is concerned with infringement on the prerogatives and authority of the clergy. With reference to the lay exhorters, the writer spoke of ''the strange Liberty some Men take of invading the Priest's Office.'' Such insolence ought to be punished by ''a total

Deprivation of the Means of Knowledge." Not only were laymen assuming the role of preachers, but, the writer said: "I have heard some Laymen pretend to judge of a Sermon, and say this and that was not agreeable to *Reason*. If these Things are not timely prevented, I dread the Event."

"Lastly," the writer said, "the most fatal Consequence of exercising REASON, is the Tendency it has to promote *Good Works,* and as these have of late been stiled, *Cursed, Abominable* and *Damnable,* I humbly conceive they ought not to be allowed in a *Christian Country*; and the most effectual Way to strike at the Commission of them, is to strike at this which is one of the chief Roots from whence they spring."

The evils which he had described were, the writer hoped, "sufficient to convince the World, that the *Word* REASON ought never to be pronounced without *Cursed*." "And for Proof of this," he said, "I appeal to the Authority and Practice of some worthy Men who are now assisting me in this Scheme."

He then proposed three methods "for the utter destruction of this *Monster.*"

The first of these proposals pertained to education. "In the first place," he said, "I would have all Male Children . . . committed to the immediate Care of old Matrons, and under that to continue 'till they are Ten Years of Age . . . ; after that they should be . . . delivered over to the Tuition of an Order of Men formed into a *private Academy,* where they should be taught to read just enough to collect News for Diversion, but by no means to learn *Hebrew, Greek* or *Latin.*" As to their reading, "they should be confined to a certain Set of Authors, and absolutely denied the *Sight* of Dr. *Tillotson,* Dr. *Clarke,* and one *Johnny Locke* in particular . . . and a few other great REASONERS whose Works have done so much Mischief in the World."

The second proposal also referred to reading. "I would," the writer said, "have all Men utterly debarred from reading the SACRED SCRIPTURES, since they give such *Encouragement* to the Use of Reason, not only by indulging us in, but commanding us to *judge* for our selves, to *examine,* to *prove all Things*; the Consequences of which are so dreadful, as must be shocking even to think of."

The third proposal was of a medical nature. "But lastly, if all these Methods should fail, I would then propose, that a skilful *Surgeon* should be appointed to prepare a *Soporifick Plaister,* to be applied to the Head directly over the *Glandular Pinealis*; for as the most profound *Anatomists* have asserted this to be the Seat of the Soul, or REASON, this part may therefore be so affected hereby as to answer the End designed in the compleatest Manner."

The writer declared in his conclusion: "These Proposals are the Result of mature Deliberation," and then ended with a promise: "If these Reflections thus thrown together may be thought to be imperfect, I shall willingly spend a little more Time in compleating this Scheme, for I am determined there shall not be a *Reasonable Creature* left (at least in this my Native Country) if it is as much in my Power to prevent it, as there seems to be an Inclination in some of my Fellow Creatures to assist me herein."

Critics of the revival not only defended reason but also attacked the excessive emotionalism which was generated by some of the preachers. Charles Chauncy, one of the ministers of the First Church in Boston, for instance, thought that the "agonies and convulsions of soul" which were experienced before conversion were unnecessary and even harmful. John Caldwell thus described the experiences that preceded what he called "supposed Conversions." "A sudden and terrible Fear of divine Wrath, or the Miseries of Hell, occasioning in some a Sensation of Cold, in most a very extraordinary Warmth all over the Body, causing people to cry as if distracted to shed tears in great Plenty; throwing many into Convulsions, and a few for some time into Despair." Regarding the second phase of the "conversion" Caldwell said: "In a few Days, or less, the Cloud blows, for ordinary, over; the Terror is at an end, and more than common Cheerfulness succeeds; all their Difficulties and Doubts are removed, and immediately a Certainty that all their sins are pardoned, and they be saved, takes place." To Caldwell the result of such experiences was unfortunate. The people who had experienced such conversion were filled with conceit about their own spiritual state and were scornful of all who had not had similar experiences.

To Jonathan Edwards the emotionalism of the revival and the attitude of the "opposers" to it provided the occasion for a philosophical consideration of the role of the "affections" in religion.

Edwards had previously, in 1734, stated his belief that the distinguishing feature of the regenerate is that they have a "true sense of the divine and superlative excellency of divine things," and that this, which is a "sense of the heart," resides, not in the understanding, but in the will or inclination of the heart. In so doing Edwards had not dismissed the understanding as useless, but had merely said that notional knowledge is less significant than the sense of the heart.

As a defender and promoter of the revival Edwards was not among those who ignored the excesses and errors. Although he acknowledged the same defects which the opposers criticized, he, more than the other writers on either side of the controversy, utilized his conceptions of human nature as a basis for explaining and excusing the errors. In so doing he used ideas and methods of reasoning that were philosophical rather than strictly theological in nature.

Edwards' first attempt to explain and defend the revival was a sermon entitled *Distinguishing Marks of a Work of the Spirit of God,* first preached as a sermon in September, 1741, and later, in expanded form, published as a small book in November. In this work, as the title indicates, Edwards stated the criteria which he thought should be used in determining whether the revival was or was not "a Work of the Spirit of God." In preparing the way for stating his positive criteria, Edwards argued that some of the characteristics of the revival to which opponents had objected were really inconclusive as evidence. It is here, in dealing with physical and mental agitation, that he used his conceptions of human nature.

"A work is not to be judged," he said, "by any effects on the bodies of men; such as tears, trembling, groans, loud outcries, agonies of body, or the failing of bodily strength. It is easily to be accounted for from the consideration of the nature of divine and eternal things, and the nature of man, and the laws of union between soul and body, how a right influence, a true and proper sense of things should have such effects on the body, even those, of the most extraordinary kind."

Turning from physical agitation to mental excitement, Edwards declared: "It is no argument that an operation on the minds of a people, is not the Work of the Spirit of God, that many who are the subjects of it, have great impressions made on their imaginations." In explanation of this, Edwards said: "Such is our nature, that we cannot think of things invisible without a degree of imagination." And, he argued, "such is our state and nature, that this faculty is really subservient and helpful to the other faculties of the mind, when a proper use is made of it; though oftentimes, when the imagination is too strong, and the other faculties weak, it overbears them in their exercises."

Edwards did not succeed in his attempt to secure a general acceptance of the revival. In the interval between his *Distinguishing Marks* and his next book, two-thirds of the pamphlets and three-fifths of the newspaper articles dealing with the revival were wholly or largely unfavorable to it. Edwards had been reading these publications and observed that none of them dealt with the revival as a whole and that the debate had been, on both sides, of such a nature that it did "not tend to bring the contention in general to an end, but rather to inflame it and increase the uproar."[2]

This second attempt to defend and promote the revival, published in March 1743, was entitled *Some Thoughts Concerning the Present Revival of Religion in New England*.

Before giving his defense, Edwards explained the reasons for "the ill thoughts" held by the opponents, in so far as they lay "in the understanding and not in the disposition" (III, 276).

One of the causes of incorrect judgments on the revival was, Edwards thought, that opponents did not make "the Holy Scripture as a *whole*, and in itself a sufficient rule to judge such things by." "Some," he asserted, "make philosophy, instead of the Holy Scripture, their rule for judging the work" (III, 279).

This philosophy which the opponents used in judging the revival was "the notions they entertain of the nature of the soul; its faculties and affections."

Edwards then proceeded to describe and criticize the conception of the affections held by the opponents, which was, in fact, the traditional view, and after that pre-

---

[2] *Works* (New York, 1844), III, 275. Subsequent references to Edwards in the present chapter are to this edition.

sented his own view of the affections and their role in religion.

On account of applying incorrect conceptions of the affections in judging the revival, "Some are willing to say, 'there is but little sober, solid religion in the work! It is little else but flash and noise. Religion now a days all runs out into transports and high flights of the passions and affections.'" Explaining the basis for this estimate of the revival Edwards said of the opponents: "In their philosophy the affections . . . are something diverse from the will, and not appertaining to the noblest part of the soul, but to the meanest principles that it has . . . as partaking of the animal nature, and what it has in common with the brute creation . . ." Although people who hold this view "acknowledge that a good use may be made of the affections, yet they suppose that the substantial part of religion does not consist in them, but that they are rather to be looked upon as something adventitious and accidental to Christianity."

Commenting on this conception, Edwards said, "I cannot but think that these gentlemen labor under great mistakes, both in philosophy and divinity." He granted, however, that discrimination must be exercised in judging "high and raised affections." "Some are," he said, "more solid than others." He was in agreement with the opponents in saying, "There are many exercises of the affections of the soul that are very flashy and little to be depended on; and oftentimes there is a great deal that appertains to them . . . that has its seat in animal nature . . ." Nevertheless, he contended that it is "false philosophy to suppose this to be the case with all exercises of the affections of the soul . . . and false divinity to suppose that religious affections do not belong to the substance and essence of Christianity." "On the contrary," Edwards declared, "it seems to me that the very life and soul of all religion consists in them" (III, 279-280).

Since Edwards had presented his views on the "sense of the heart" in his sermon of 1734 and his views on the emotions in his *Distinguishing Marks* of 1741, he had apparently elaborated his conceptions of the human mind. Now, in order to support his assertion regarding the role of the affections in religion, he defined and explained the affections in a way that gave them a higher rating than they had had in the traditional view, which was the one held by critics of the revival.

It was a mistake, Edwards declared, to think that "the affections of the soul are something diverse from the will." Then, stating his own theory, he said: "I humbly conceive that the affections of the soul are not properly distinguished from the will, as though they were two faculties." In support of his conception of the identity of the will and the affections, he gave the following argument: "All acts of the affections of the soul are in some sense acts of the will, and all acts of the will are acts of the affections. All exercises of the will are in some degree or other, exercise of the soul's appetition or aversion; or which is the same thing, of its love or hatred. The soul wills one thing rather than another, or chooses one thing rather than another, no otherwise than it loves one thing more than another; but love and hate are affections of the soul: And therefore all acts of the will are truly acts of the affections." Then, to explain why, although the will and the affections are one and the same, different terms were used, he said that "the exercises of the will do not obtain the name of passions, unless the will, either in its aversion or opposition, be exercised in a high degree, or in a vigorous and lively manner" (III, 280).

Thus, in identifying the affections with the will, Edwards had, he supposed, given them a higher standing than was ordinarily accorded them, since the will had always been given a high rating along with the understanding.

Although Edwards had thus elevated the standing of the affections and had said that the "very life and soul of all true religion consists in them," he granted that there is "a great deal of difference in high and raised affections which must be distinguished by the skill of the observer." For distinguishing between genuine and fake religious affections, criteria were needed. In the winter of 1742-1743, while he was writing *Some Thoughts,* Edwards preached a series of sermons which provided such criteria. These sermons were not published and the manuscripts are not extant. The substance of them was, however, later reworked and, shortly after the end of the revival, published in a book entitled *A Treatise Concerning Religious Affections.* This book, based on the concept of the affections proposed in *Some Thoughts,* was judged, with reference to both its quality and its influence, one of the most important of Edwards' works and represents the most significant theological outcome of the Great Awakening.

Charles Chauncy read Edwards' *Some Thoughts* immediately after its publication and at once advertised a plan for a book entitled *Seasonable Thoughts on the State of Religion in New England* as a reply. There were, he thought, things in Edwards' book which made it dangerous.

Chauncy had been one of the critics of the revival who never acknowledged that it had had any good effects at all. In previous sermons and pamphlets he had taken up a few of what he considered the errors attending the revival. His *Seasonable Thoughts* was both a comprehensive criticism of the revival and a reply to Edwards' *Some Thoughts.*

The basic difference between Edwards and Chauncy

lay in their attitudes toward the affections and the understanding. Edwards, as has been seen, had declared that the "very life and soul of all true religion consists in the affections." Chauncy, on the other hand, said: "A Judgment has been too commonly formed of Men's *spiritual* Condition more from their *Affections*, than the *permanent Temper* of their Minds discovered in the habitual *Conduct* of their Lives; not duly considering, how precarious that Religion must be, which has its *Rise* from the *Passions*, and not any thorow *Change* in the *Understanding* and Will" (pp. 2-3). Chauncy was obviously one of those who held the view of the affections which Edwards attributed to the opposers. He was apparently unconvinced by the attempt to prove that the affections and the will are identical, since he considers conversion to be a *"Change* in the *Understanding* and *Will,"* and mentions the "Passions" separately, and considers that a "Religion . . . which has its Rise from the *Passions"* is very "precarious." From this point of view Chauncy devoted many pages of his book to descriptions of emotional excesses and disorders in the revival meetings. For these he did not, like Edwards, find any palliative explanations by considering the facts of human nature.

After displaying the effects of emotional preaching, Chauncy proclaimed: "The plain Truth is, an *enlightened Mind* and not *raised Affections,* ought always to be the Guide of those who call themselves Men: and this, in the Affairs of Religion, as well as other Things" (pp. 326-327).

Edwards, as has been seen, had introduced his defense of the affections in a passage which began with the complaint that "Some make *Philosophy,* INSTEAD of the holy Scriptures their rule of Judging of this Work; particularly, the *philosophical* Notions they entertain of the Nature of the Soul, its Faculties and Affections."

In reply to this complaint, Chauncy said: "If no Use might be made of *Philosophy*, in explaining the Scripture, how monstrous must our Conceptions of the infinite GOD be, while he is represented, according to the *Letter* of numberless *Texts*, as having *Eyes*, and *Ears*, and *Hands* and *Feet*; and as being subject to the various Passions of *Love*, and *Hatred*; *Joy* and *Grief*; *Anger*, *Wrath, Revenge*, and the like?" "We must," he declared, "be allowed the Exercise of our *Reason*, (which is but another Name for what is here meant by *Philosophy*) or we shall be liable to be wretchedly impos'd on by our Imaginations: Nor is there any Error, however extravagant, but we shall be in Danger of falling into it." "If we give up our Understanding," he asked, "how shall we be able to ascertain the Sense of any one Text of Scripture? What should hinder our running into all the Wilds of Delusion?" Then, with reference to Edwards, Chauncy observed, "But this use of *Philosophy*, I conclude this *Gentleman* will not object against." "If he does," he said, "I see not but he will be self-condemn'd; for he has himself, under this very Head, made use of more *Philosophy* (and in a Manner not altogether exceptionable, as we may see afterwards, if I can find Room) than any one that I know, who has wrote upon the Times." Presumably Chauncy, in reminding Edwards that he himself had used philosophy, was referring to his discussion of the affections. It is regrettable that he did not "find room" for the examination of Edwards' views which he tentatively promised. Although he granted that Edwards' use of philosophy was not "altogether exceptionable," it seems clear from the general tenor of his book that he would have taken exception to Edwards' high estimate of the affections themselves and of their role in religion. At any rate, he closed this part of his reply to Edwards by denying the charge that because some people thought that "Religion now-Days all runs out into Transports, and high Flights of the Passions and Affections, it hence follows, that they make Phylosophy (INSTEAD of *Scripture*) their Rule of Judging in this Matter" (pp. 383-384).

Chauncy did not, however, completely condemn the emotions, although he distrusted them. After devoting the major portion of his book to adverse criticism of the revival and of Edwards' defense of it, he concluded a section "Directing more positively to what may be judged the best Expedients to promote the Interest of Religion at this Day."

Among his proposals there was one which pertained to the role of the emotions in religion. "A wrong Use of the Passions, in the Business of Religion, is . . .," he said, "a Matter highly needful to be guarded against at this Day. There is, no Doubt, a good Use to be made of the Passions.— —They were not in vain planted in our Nature;— —but because wisely adapted to serve many Purposes, in the *religious* as well as the *natural* Life.— But they are capable of being *abused,* and have actually been so; as is abundantly evident from many of the Disorders prevailing in these times" (pp. 418-419). "Instances of the Abuse of the Passions . . . have not been wanting in these Times; Nor unless some Persons are made sensible of it, and take care to keep their Passions within the Restraints of Reason, may it be expected that Things should be reduced to a state of Order? There is," he concluded, "the Religion of the *Understanding* and *Judgment* and *Will,* as well as of the Affections; and if little Account is made of the *former,* while great stress is made of the *latter,* it can't be but People should run into Disorders" (p. 422).

Chauncy ended his list of recommendations with an appeal for independent thinking—for the use of reason —in matters of religion. "The last Thing I shall mention as necessary, at this Day," he said, "is a due Care to *prove all Things,* that we may *hold fast to that which is good.* . . . And, perhaps, there never was a Time when a Regard to this Advice was more needful. We have seen enough to convince us, that . . . the Determinations, whether of *single Persons,* or of *public Bodies of Men* . . . are not to be received with an *implicit Faith.*— If we would act up to our Character as Men, or Christians, we must not submit blindfold to the Dictates of others. . . . Nor can we be too solicitous, so far as we are able, to see with our own Eyes, and believe with our own Understandings" (pp. 423-424).

Chauncy followed his own advice throughout his career. Although his later writings contain little that is technically philosophical, they exemplify his own definition of philosophy as "the Exercise of our Reason." Chauncy became the outstanding example of a rationalistic liberalism which completely repudiated Calvinism.

Edwards, on the other hand, later made extensive use of philosophical conceptions in support of Calvinistic doctrines which were being menaced by the growth of liberalism.

The revival, after a long period of decline, finally came to an end as an effective movement in the fall of 1745. For its ending Edwards found a reason in the facts of human nature: men are prone to run from one extreme to another.

III

JONATHAN EDWARDS ON THE EMOTIONS

Excessive emotionalism had posed a problem for judicious supporters of the revival and a basis for criticism by the opponents. During the revival Jonathan Edwards had presented his conception of the affections and their role in religion. These ideas he carried over into the period after the Awakening and in the spring of 1746 he published *A Treatise concerning Religious Affections*. The condition which he now faced was totally different from that which existed when he wrote his books in support of the revival. Comparing the present situation with that of the recent past, Edwards observed that "instead of esteeming and admiring all religious affections without distinction, it is a thing much more prevalent to reject and discard all without distinction" (p. 119). This attitude, Edwards deplored. "The prevailing prejudice against religious affections at this day, in the land, is apparently of awful effect, to harden the hearts of sinners, and damp the graces of many of the saints, and stunt the life and power of religion . . . and hold us down in a state of dulness and apathy . . ." Still solicitous about the reputation of the revival, Edwards feared that this prejudice against religious affections "undoubtedly causes many persons greatly to offend God, in entertaining mean and low thoughts of the extraordinary work he has lately wrought in the land" (p. 121).[1]

The philosophical content of the *Treatise* is mainly psychological, ethical, and esthetic.

Edwards laid the foundation for his treatment of the role of the emotions in religion by restating his psychological ideas. The soul, he again said, has two faculties: the understanding and the will, or inclination. By the understanding, the soul "discerns, and views and judges of things." But "the soul does not merely perceive and view things." It is either "inclined *to* them, or is disinclined and averse *from* them." When this inclination governs and determines action "it is called the will." The affections are not a distinct and separate faculty, but are "no other, than the more vigorous and sensible

---

[1] All quotations from the *Treatise* are from the edition by John E. Smith, Yale University Press, 1959.

exercises of the inclination and will of the soul" (pp. 96-97).

Regarding the role of the emotions in human affairs in general, Edwards said: "Such is man's nature, that he is very unactive, any otherwise than he is influenced by some affection. . . . These affections we see to be the springs that set men a going in all the affairs of life, and engage them in all their pursuits: these are the things that put men forward, and carry them along, in all their worldly business." Likewise, Edwards thought, "in religious matters the spring of [men's] actions are very much religious affections: he that has doctrinal knowledge . . . only, without affection, never is engaged in the business of religion" (p. 101).

On this basis is established the fundamental thesis of the book: "True religion, in great part, consists in holy affections" (p. 95).

This, however, presents a problem: "There are false affections, and there are true. A man's having much affection, does not prove that he has any true religion: but if he has not affection, it proves that he has no true religion. The right way is not to reject all affections, nor to approve all; but to distinguish between affections, approving some, and rejecting others . . ." (p. 121).

In preparation for giving the criteria for making such distinctions, Edwards devoted a long section of his book to showing "what are no certain signs that religious affections are truly gracious, or that they are not" (p. 125). In doing this he touched upon several of the features of the revival which had been subjects for controversy. He said, for instance, "It is no sign one way or another, that religious affections are very great, or raised very high" (p. 127). Of another of the inconclusive matters, he said, "It is no sign that affections have the nature of true religion, or that they have not, that they have great effects on the body." In explanation of this he added: "Such are the laws of union of soul and body that the mind can have no lively or vigorous exercises, without some effect upon the body." No rule can be found, however, for determining whether the affections that produce these effects are spiritual. "None," Edwards observed, "has been found in all the late controversies which have been about things of this nature" (pp. 131-132).

Having prepared the way by this explanation of his theory of the affections and by dismissing the inconclusive "signs," Edwards proceeded with his main purpose by stating and discussing twelve "signs of gracious affections." Of these, six are the most significant in themselves and also because of their later influence. In presenting these criteria, Edwards made considerable use of ideas he had already stated in his youthful *Notes on the Mind* and in his sermon on *A Divine and Supernatural Light*.

The first of these "signs" is: "Affections that are truly spiritual and gracious do arise from those influences and operations on the heart, which are spiritual, supernatural and divine" (p. 197). The result of these operations on the heart is that "in those gracious exercises and affections which are wrought in the minds of the saints ... there is a new inward perception or sensation of their minds, entirely different in its nature and kind, from any thing that ever their minds were the subject of before they were sanctified" (p. 205). After this change "something is perceived by a true saint, in the exercise of this new sense of mind, in spiritual and divine things, as entirely diverse from any thing that is perceived in them by natural men, as the sweet taste of honey is diverse from ideas men have of honey by only looking on it, and feeling of it." Edwards insisted, however, that "this new spiritual sense and the new dispositions that attend it, are no new faculties, but new principles of nature" (p. 206).

In those who have been given this new sense, the object and the motive of the affections are changed. Thus the second of Edwards' signs is: "The first objective ground of gracious affections, is the transcendentally excellent and amiable nature of divine things, as they are in themselves; and not any conceived relation they bear to self or self-interest" (p. 240). Men can, Edwards thought, profess love of God for what they conceive he has done for them. This is mere gratitude and is a sign of self-love. The love of the saints, on the other hand, arises from "the excellency of divine things, as they are in themselves, and not from any conceived relationship they bear to their interest" (p. 249).

In stating the third sign Edwards defined more precisely the nature of the "excellency" of the divine things which are the object of the saints' affections. "Those affections that are truly holy, are," he said, "founded on the loveliness of the moral excellency of divine things. Or . . . a love to divine things for the beauty and sweetness of their moral excellency is the first beginning and spring of all holy affections" (pp. 253-254). In connection with this "sign" Edwards stated the basic doctrines of his own moral philosophy. Since he considered that the "moral excellency" of divine things is the object of the saints' affections and that the affections are exercises of the will, he asserted that the "moral excellency" of man "is more immediately seated in the heart or will . . ." If a man's "will is truly right and lovely, he is morally good or excellent." Such moral excellence is holiness, and, Edwards declared, "there is no other true virtue, but true holiness" (p. 255). The conception that virtue is seated in the will and that only holiness is true virtue is characteristic not only of Edwards but also of his followers and later brought them into conflict with the moderate Calvinists of New England.

In the fourth "sign" relations between the affections and the understanding are involved. "Gracious affections," Edwards said, "do arise from the mind's being enlightened, richly and spiritually to understand or apprehend divine things." In explanation of this point, he declared, "Holy affections are not heat without light; but evermore arise from the information of the understanding, some spiritual instruction that the mind receives, light or actual knowledge" (p. 266).

In discussing apprehension of divine things Edwards described two ways of forming judgments. In doing this he made use of esthetic ideas. In his "Notes on the Mind" he had dealt with the properties of beautiful objects. Now he is concerned also with the nature of the perception of beauty. In his sermon on *A Divine and Supernatural Light* and again in the present book, he dwells on the sense of divine things. To clarify this idea of the spiritual sense, Edwards made use of a parallel between esthetic taste and spiritual taste as exercised in forming judgments. "There is," he said, "such a thing as good taste of natural beauty . . . that is exercised about temporal things, in judging of them; as about the justness of a speech, the goodness of style, the beauty of a poem . . . " Then, quoting from the article on taste in Ephraim Chambers' *Cyclopaedia, or an Universal Dictionary of Arts and Sciences* (1728), he added "To have a taste is to give things their real value, to be touched with the good, to be shocked with the ill . . . Taste and judgment, then, should be the same thing; and yet it is easy to discern a difference. The judgment forms its opinions from reflection; the reason on this occasion fetches a kind of circuit, to arrive at its end, it supposes principles, it draws consequences, and it judges; but not without a thorough knowledge of the case. . . . Good taste observes none of these formalities; ere it has had time to consult; it has taken its side; as soon as ever the object is presented it the impression is made, the sentiment is formed . . ." Then, describing a similar process in spiritual judgments, he continued: "Now, as there is such a kind of taste of mind as this, which philosophers speak of . . . so there is such a thing as a divine taste . . . in the hearts of the saints, whereby they are in like manner led and guided in discerning and distinguishing the true spiritual and holy beauty of actions . . ." (pp. 282-283).

The function of the spiritual sense in the formation of judgments about religious matters is also illustrated by an esthetic parallel in Edwards' fifth "sign." "Truly gracious affections are attended with a reasonable and spiritual conviction of the judgment, of the reality and certainty of divine things" (p. 292), but this conviction is not achieved solely by an intellectual process. "He that truly sees the divine, transcendental, supreme glory of those things that are divine, does, as it were, know their divinity intuitively: he not only argues that they are divine but he sees that they are divine" (p. 298). To support this statement, Edwards made use of a comparison between the recognition of literary merit and the recognition of religious truths. "There is," he said, "need of uncommon force of mind to discern the distinguishing excellencies of the works of authors of great genius: those things in Milton, which to mean judges appear tasteless and imperfections, are his inimitable excellencies in the eyes of those who are of greater discerning and better taste." Just as men of inferior literary discernment cannot appreciate the qualities of Milton's poetry, so the unregenerate cannot properly discern the spiritual matters contained in the Bible. "And if there be a book, which God is the author of, it is most reasonable to suppose, that the distinguishing glories of his word are of such a kind, as that the sin and corruption of men's hearts . . . which . . . makes the heart dull and stupid to any sense or taste of those things wherein the moral glory of the divine perfections consists; I say . . . that this would blind men from discerning the beauties of such a book; and that therefore they will not see them but as God is pleased to enlighten them, and restore an holy taste, to discern and relish divine beauties" (p. 301).

Edwards expressed his tenth criterion in esthetic terms and in the exposition of it used a concept which he had stated long before in his "Notes on the Mind," in which he had said that "all Excellency is *Harmony, Symmetry,* or *Proportion.*" Harmony among spirits he identified as love. Utilizing this concept in his present undertaking, he continued, "Another thing wherein those affections that are truly gracious and holy, differ from those that are false, is beautiful symmetry and proportion" (p. 365). He proceeded to show how love—which is the essence of harmony among spirits—is bestowed by unregenerate hypocrites without regard to proper proportion. There are some who "make high pretences, and a great shew of love to God and Christ . . . but they have not a spirit of love and benevolence towards men . . . And, on the other hand, there are others, that appear as if they had a great deal of benevolence to men . . . but have no love to God." "And as to love to men, there are some whose affections are not of so universal a nature, as a truly Christian love is." "They are full of dear affections to some, and full of bitterness toward others." In this there is a "monstrous disproportion." Another kind of disproportion is found in the fact that "some men shew a love to others as to their outward man, they are liberal of their worldly substance, and often give to the poor; but have no love to, or concern for the souls of men." "Others," on the other hand, "pretend a great love to men's souls, that are not compassionate and charitable towards their bodies." The reason for this is that "making a great shew of love, pity and distress for souls, cost them nothing; but in order to shew mercy to men's bodies, they must part with money out of their pockets. . . . A true Christian love to our brethren extends both to their bodies and souls" (pp. 368-369).

The Great Awakening had created serious divisions among the clergy and people of New England. Edwards' treatise on the affections, in turn, contributed to still another one. His elevation of the will and its related affections over the understanding, his insistence that a sense of divine things is superior to a notional knowledge of them, and his identification of true virtue with holiness provided the starting point for a school of theology at first called the New Divinity and later Hopkinsianism. This divinity carried the traditional Calvinistic tenets to rigorous doctrinal extremes which were opposed by the moderate Calvinists among the Congregational clergy.

Certainly the revival and its consequences had presented problems not only to the Congregationalists but to the Anglicans as well. Among the latter the most important man who considered these problems was Samuel Johnson.

IV

SAMUEL JOHNSON
CHURCHMAN AND PHILOSOPHER

After the conversion of Johnson and his friends, other Yale men followed him into the Church of England. This produced consternation among the Congregationalists of

New England, and as a result there was a prolonged controversy in the 1720's and 1730's in which Johnson and others defended Episcopal church polity and the usages of the Church of England against criticisms by Congregational ministers.

During the revival the Anglicans published nothing until it had virtually run its course. The revival did, however, present both a problem and an opportunity to them which Johnson described in letters to ecclesiastical authorities in England. He feared the possible effect of revivalistic preaching on the people, but he also thought that the excesses might encourage some of them to find a haven in the Church of England.

On September 29, 1741, after the revival had been in progress about a year, Johnson, in a letter dealing with church affairs addressed to the Archbishop of Canterbury, wrote: "I will only add that the exigensies of the church in these parts at this time are very particular by reason of the great progress of the most odd and unaccountable enthusiasm that perhaps ever obtained in any age or nation. For not only the minds of many people are at once struck with prodigious distresses upon those hideous outcries of a set of itinerant preachers that go up and down among us, but even their bodies are frequently in a moment affected with the strangest convulsions and involuntary agitations, which have sometimes happened without their minds being affected at all. The church has not as yet much suffered but has in many instances gained by these strange commotions." With regard to protecting and promoting the interests of the Church in these circumstances, Johnson wrote: "But in order to this it is not only necessary that we who are in the Society's service take much care and pains among the people, but also if possible that there be more laborers sent into the harvest" (III, 228-229).

In his semi-annual report to Philip Bearcroft, Secretary of the Society for the Propagation of the Gospel, written a few days later, Johnson referred the secretary to this passage in the letter to the Archbishop and added, "As to my own people, they have hitherto been preserved entirely from this contagion while the Dissenters of this parish are pretty much infected, of whom several seem very likely to be about retiring into the Church" (III, 229).

In his next report to the Society for the Propagation of the Gospel, dated March 25, 1742, Johnson wrote: "Since my last the raging enthusiasm which I then mentioned has much prevailed in this country among the Dissenters and appears in many of them like a kind of epidemical frenzy attended with several strange doctrines ... destructive of all religion. . . . But thank God the Church save one or two instances has been yet preserved and the distractions of the times have in many instances been improved to open people's eyes and awaken their attention towards the Church as their only refuge to which four good families have since my last been entirely reconciled, and several others seem likely to follow them." Then, telling of the efforts required to meet the situation, Johnson said: "But in order to prevent the mischief and make an advantage of it we are obliged to be continually riding and preaching. I have scarce ever failed all this winter of preaching three times, frequently four times, and sometimes five or six times in a week, and this often not only in this town but in divers other parts of the colony. And there is this advantage arising from the madness of the times that it does remarkably engage people's attention to our preaching and administrations" (III, 230-231).

Explaining further the threat to the Church of England in New England, Johnson continued: "But it would be endless to tell of the dreams and visions, ecstasies, trances, revelations and conversions attended with fall-

ings, swoonings, convulsions, terrors, joys, assurances
and I know not what, together with endless confusion,
lying and misrepresentation especially of the Church
which the country is everywhere full of, while at the
same time their indefatigable endeavours are used to
unhinge all public order, so that it looks as if these
enthusiasts would shortly get the government into their
hands and tyrannize over us . . . '' (III, 231).

A few months later, on October 5, 1742, Johnson observed, in a report to the Secretary of the Society for
the Propagation of the Gospel, that there had been a
change for the better. ''The enthusiasm I gave you an
account of in my last has somewhat abated, which has
been occasioned by the foolish and vicious conduct of
some of their teachers, who have been discovered to go
into some very odd familiarities with the women. The
Church has been so far from losing that it has considerably gained by the accession of three or four good
families'' (III, 232).

Except for their concern about the welfare of the
Church of England, the Anglicans obviously agreed with
the opposers among the Congregationalists in their estimate of the revival, but none of the sermons which the
Anglicans preached to counteract the effects of the revival when it was at its height in 1742 were published.

In 1745, however, at the very end of the revival, two
Anglican sermons were published which dealt with issues
connected with the revival, and Johnson published a
pamphlet in which he attacked the Calvinistic theological position.

A sermon entitled *The True Nature of Christian
Preaching*, by Henry Caner, was obviously intended as
an antidote to the emotional preaching of the revivalists.
''And should we address the passions only,'' Caner said,
''it would be a shameful betraying of our trust.'' Stating
the Anglican attitude toward emotionalism, he declared:

"It has been the Glory of our Church always to oppose itself to such Excesses, whether they arise from superstition, or . . . from weakness of Understanding;" and concerning the function of the preacher: "Our chief Province . . . is with the Understanding. This we may inform, this we may enlighten, this we may instruct and convince." Also he emphasized that preaching should provide mainly moral instruction and complained that such preaching was often scornfully described "as legal Preaching, carnal Instruction, preaching Morality."

The Anglicans objected not only to the emotionalism of the revivalists, but also to their Calvinistic doctrines. John Beach dealt with the doctrine of election in *A Sermon, Shewing that Eternal Life is God's Gift, Bestowed upon All Men who Obey the Gospell. And that Free Grace and Free Will Concur, in the Affair of Man's Salvation* (1745). Stating a view of election that differed sharply from the Calvinistic doctrine, Beach said that all Christians are elected, just as all Hebrews had been a chosen people, but that they must exert effort "to make their calling and election sure." This effort is necessary and possible because they have free will. Regarding the will, Beach, in a statement which was distinctly at variance with Calvinistic doctrine, asserted: "Though man is a fallen, weak creature, yet there is in everyone a power of self-determining, of chusing, or refusing; by which a man can comply with or reject the suggestions of the holy Spirit. . . . And if once you take away freedom of will from man, you degrade him from being a moral agent into an unintelligent machine."

Johnson had, in his reports on the revival, given special attention to the excesses and disorders. He was also, however, disturbed by the Calvinistic doctrines of the revivalists, particularly their concept of God's sovereignty and the doctrine of election. He therefore published in 1745 a pamphlet entitled *A Letter from Aris-*

tocles to Authades Concerning the Sovereignty and Promises of God, which he had written in September, 1744. Although it was not published until the revival had run its course, it was, he said, written at a "time when the enthusiasm was rampant, which placed all in predestination and mere sovereignty." In the "Advertisement" to the *Letter* itself, Johnson said: "What prevailed on me to consent to the publishing of the following letter, was a sincere and firm persuasion, that it is really the cause of God and Christ that I here plead, and that the eternal interest of the souls of men is very nearly concerned in it. For it is manifest to me, that some notions have of late been propagated and inculcated in this country, that are equally destructive to the right belief of both God and the Gospel." But "I am not insensible that the odious name of Arminianism will be the cry against these papers" (III, 162).

In the beginning of the *Letter* Johnson represents himself as having had a conversation with Authades, a strict Calvinist, who asked: "You may remember, it was your chief inquiry, as a test of my being a true Christian, can you in sincerity subscribe to the truth of our doctrine? By which you meant the doctrine of the divine sovereignty, as you had explained it: *i.e.,* if I understand you right, as implying God's eternal, arbitrary and absolute determination of the everlasting fate of his creatures, from his own mere notion, and without any consideration of their good or ill behavior." The answer of Aristides (Johnson) to the question was "No, good Sir, by no means." It is, he said, contrary to many texts and to the general drift of Scripture and also "utterly contrary to the divine attributes" (III, 162-163).

"It is," he continued, "contrary to the nature and attributes of God, because it appears plainly inconsistent with the very notion of his being a moral governor of the world: for it represents Him as laying his creatures under a necessity of being what they are, whether good or bad, and so leaves no room for either virtue or vice, praise or blame, reward or punishment, properly speaking" (III, 163).

This Calvinistic view of sovereignty, Johnson thought, tends "not only to tempt us to entertain hard and unworthy thoughts of God, but also to cut the sinews of all our endeavors to repent and return to Him and our duty . . . since, for aught we know, we may be absolutely excluded from all possibility of succeeding by a sovereign and inexorable decree of reprobation" (III, 164).

Of the effect of the Anglican conception of God, however, he said: "Whereas on the contrary, nothing can so effectually tend to put us upon the most vigorous exertion of ourselves in endeavoring to be holy as God is holy, righteous as He is righteous . . ., as those most amiable apprehensions of him, which represent him as being an universal lover of the souls which he hath made, and sincerely and solicitously desirous of their happiness, in proportion to their several capacities . . . to grant them all the aid and assistance necessary thereunto, so far as can consist with his treating them as being what they are, and what he himself hath made them." Johnson described men as being "tho' frail, yet free, self-exerting and self-determining agents." God therefore makes "all the tender and merciful allowances for their frailty that can consist with the sincerity of their obedience, and his righteousness and authority in the government of the world." "And this, I think, is," Johnson added, "manifestly the idea or conception of God, which (agreeably to the light of nature) the Holy Scriptures universally give us concerning him" (III, 164).

In the Calvinistic view unconditional election to salvation or damnation was a necessary exercise of God's sovereignty. In line with his conception of the divine attributes, Johnson gave Authades a description of sovereignty, which, he said, "is widely different from yours." "And in order to think clearly on this subject ...," he said, "it seems to me very necessary to distinguish between the consideration of God as a benefactor and as a judge ... In the one God acts as a sovereign lord of his favors, and in the other as a righteous judge of the behavior of his creatures under them." God is, Johnson thought, "entirely sovereign as a benefactor in the distribution of his talents and favors, both spiritual and temporal, as a proper means of trial and probation in this world: *i.e.*, the various abilities, capacities, privileges and advantages He bestoweth upon mankind." As a judge, God will treat each man "according to his conduct in the use of the talent that was committed to his trust" (III, 165-166). As to the future life, "God's decrees with regard to that state can imply nothing else but his resolution to treat all men according to the use they shall have made of his several allotments to them in this world" (III, 168).

Johnson also disagreed with the Calvinists in another point related to their conception of the decrees. According to the Westminster Confession, "By the decree of God, for the manifestation of His glory, some men ... are predestinated unto everlasting life, and others foreordained to everlasting death." Not only was Johnson's conception of the decrees at variance with the Calvinistic doctrine, but his conception of God's purpose with reference to man was also accordingly different. "As therefore," he said, "God has thus plainly discovered his decrees to be such as the facts in conjunction with his attributes and revealed religion declare them to be ... so I conceive that his great end in giving being to his creatures, and in all his various dispensations to-

109

wards them must have been (not any self-views; not to serve himself of them, or to add anything to his own happiness, for he is infinitely self-sufficient for that, independent on any of his creatures,) but that they might be happy in proportion to their several capacities, talents and improvements, in consequence of their cheerfull submission to his sovereign allotments, and sincere and faithful obedience to all his holy and righteous laws . . ." (III, 170-171).

Although Johnson had obviously used philosophical thinking in describing the attributes of God, he had, he said, set aside "all metaphysics and words without any meaning . . . which have nothing to do with the present subject" (III, 161). He attributed the false views of the Calvinists to the fact that their whole system was "not founded on the Holy Scripture (taken as a whole, and critically read and considered) but on the empty cobwebs of scholastical metaphysics (vain philosophy, science falsely so-called) together with some few obscure texts, not rightly understood. . . ." (III, 180).

Johnson was here repudiating *vain* philosophy and not philosophy as such. Although this pamphlet was not itself specifically philosophical, it contained some of the religious sentiments which were to be an integral part of two philosophical works, one of which was published in the next year, 1746.

This work was a short treatise on ethics entitled *A System of Morality* designed as a textbook. Johnson also had in mind a broader purpose—to call attention to the threats to morality in the time immediately after the revival.

During the revival the evangelistic preachers had been emphatic in declaring that good works before conversion are of no avail with reference to justification, and neglected the standard doctrine that after conversion good works, although not the cause, are evidence of justification. The reaction against a religion of mere morality had sometimes reached the opposite extreme—Antinomianism, according to which with the coming of Christ the moral law as well as the ceremonial law of the Jews had been superseded. Believing that this attitude toward morality had persisted after the revival, Johnson said with reference to his book: "Such a short delineation of morals, may, perhaps, be of some use, especially in these times, wherein there is a sect arisen, or rather revived, that is continually decrying morality, as tho' it were only carnal reason, and no part of Christianity, nor scarce consistent with it. This, it may be presumed, they would scarcely do, if they duly considered what morality truly is" (II, 443).

Johnson also feared that morality might at the same time be endangered by skepticism. "And, on the other hand," he said, "as one extreme is apt to beget another, it is to be feared there may be another sect arisen, or gaining ground, who from too just an indignation at those absurd notions of Christianity, are in danger, for want of due consideration, of not only setting light by that, but even of losing all serious sense of the true extent and obligations of morality itself."

On account of this double threat to morality, therefore, it was his "design . . . to endeavor to give a just notion of it, and the reasons on which it is founded, and to show its extent and importance, and what connection there is between it and Christianity " (II, 444).

Stating his intention and his point of view more particularly, he continued: "What is here attempted is a short system of ethics and morals . . . which have of late been called The Religion of Nature; by which I would not be understood to mean a system of truths and duties which mere natural reason would ever, of itself, have discovered, in the present condition of mankind, without the assistance of revelation or instruction. . . .

111

What I would therefore be understood to mean by Ethics, or the Religion of Nature, is, that system of truths and duties, wh.ch, tho' they are not obvious to our weak reason, without revelation or instruction, yet when discovered . . . do evidently appear . . . to be founded in the first principles of reason and nature; in the nature of God and man, and the various relations that subsist between them; and from thence to be capable of strict demonstration" (II, 442-443).

In *A Letter from Aristocles to Authades* Johnson had declared that man's happiness is God's chief concern. Now, as a moral philosopher, Johnson demonstrated how man can achieve the happiness for which he was intended. "Ethics," he said, "is the art of living happily, by the right knowledge of ourselves, and the practice of virtue: our happiness being the end, and knowledge and virtue, the means to that end." Happiness Johnson defines as "that pleasure which ariseth in us from the enjoyment of ourselves, and all that is really good for us, or suitable to our natures, and conducive to our happiness in the whole." "The enjoyment of ourselves, and all that is truly good, depends on a good habit, or state of the soul, united with, and delighting in its proper objects, which are truth and good." Truth is "the object of the understanding" and good is "the object of the will and affections." Being united with and delighting in these two objects "is the same thing with virtue" (II, 446-447).

The basic doctrine of his treatise was stated thus: "Morality . . . is the same thing with the Religion of Nature, or that religion which is founded in the nature of things." With reference to practice, "it may be defined, the pursuit of our true happiness by thinking, affecting and acting, according to the laws of truth and right reason, under a sense of the duty that we owe to Almighty God, and the account we must expect to give

112

of ourselves to Him." "Since therefore truth and duty
are thus necessarily connected, it must be our business
in this essay to search out all the truths that relate both
to ourselves, to God, and our fellow creatures, and
thence to deduce the several duties that do necessarily
result from them" (II, 452).

Johnson then put in the form of questions in the first
person six topics which he intended to cover in the
treatise.

"I. What am I? II. How came I to be what I am?
III. For what end was I made and have my being? IV.
What ought I immediately to do, and be, in order to
answer the end of my being? V. Whether I am what I
ought to be? If not, VI. What ought I to do, as a means,
in order to be and do what I ought, and in order finally
to answer the end of my being?" "The three first of
these enquiries," he observed, "will discover the truths;
and the three last, the duties, that we are concerned
to know and do in order to our true happiness. And the
truths are the speculative, and the duties are the practical part of moral philosophy" (II, 453).

In accordance with his plan, Johnson divided the main
body of his treatise into two parts: I. The speculative
part of moral philosophy: II. The practical part of moral
philosophy.

In Part I, he answered the first three of his six questions. The answer to the question, "What am I?" is
given in a chapter entitled "Of the Nature of Man, his
Excellencies and Imperfections."

Man recognizes that he has certain "sensations, appetites, and exertions" in common with animals. "But
then," he says of himself, "I am conscious of vastly
nobler powers and faculties than these. For I find I can
reflect and look into my own mind, and consider myself
and my own powers and actions, and their objects. I
can attend to the light of the pure intellect, and compare

one thing with another, and observe their several relations, and abstract and give names. I can judge of true and false, and of right and wrong, and deliberate and weigh things, and reason and infer one thing from another, and reduce them into method and order, according to their various connections and dependences. I can excite imaginations and conceptions of things past or absent, and recollect them in my mind at pleasure, and reject or keep them under my consideration as I please, at least in a good measure, and am at liberty to suspend judging till I have carefully examined them, and to act, or not to act, in consequence of my deliberations, as I think fit. In the impressions of sense indeed, and the perceptions of evidence, I am passive, but in all these I am evidently active, and can choose or refuse, will or nill, act or forbear, from a principle of self-exertion; which are all truly great and noble powers" (II, 455).

Such is a man within himself considered solely as an individual. But he also perceives that he has relations with others. "As to those of my own species . . . I find we were evidently made for society, being furnished with the power of speech as well as reason, whereby we are capable of entering into the understanding of each other's minds and sentiments . . . and jointly conspiring to promote our common well-being; to which we are naturally led by a principle of benevolence, and social dispositions and affections, founded in the frame and condition of our nature, which . . . lays us under a necessity of mutual dependence one upon another, which obligeth us to enter into compacts for our defense and safety, and for maintaining both private right and public order, and promoting the common good of our species, in the several communities to which we belong" (II, 458).

114

Although man's "powers" are "great and noble," they are limited and imperfect.

"My sight and hearing are very scanty; my understanding is but small; my conceptions are very feeble; my memory is very brittle; my attention is very weak; my knowledge is very confused; my will is very irresolute; my power is very infirm, and my activity can extend but to a very small compass" (II, 459).

Not only are our powers limited, "but, which is worse, . . . we are troubled with some unhappy tendency or other, in the frame of our nature; some idle sensual disposition; some importunate appetite, or some untoward passion, which it is very difficult to keep within reasonable bounds, and in indulgence to which, it is much if we have not contracted some ill habit or other . . . for which our reason and consciences have sadly reproached us, and given us very great uneasiness, and sometimes terrible aprehensions and forebodings of vengeance to come, unless we repent and reform" (II, 459).

"Such a strange mixture is human nature! Such a various creature is man! Such his noble abilities and excellencies on the one hand, and such his imperfections on the other" (II, 460).

Johnson answered the question, "How came I to be what I am?" in a chapter entitled "Of the Author of our Nature, His Perfections and Operations."

From his consciousness of his own existence and his own characteristics, man can arrive at knowledge of the being and attributes of God. He thus concludes that the being who is the cause of his existence "must, Himself, have understanding, knowledge, will, force, and activity; must have liberty, choice, deliberation, self-exertion and self-determination; and must be a being of equity, justice and goodness, and all other moral perfections, which are implied in these, and which are comprehended under the terms holiness and rectitude" (II, 462).

115

Man can learn of the being and attributes of God not only by considering his own existence and characteristics. These things "may be also demonstrated from the existence of every sensible thing that I see, hear and feel from without me." In explanation of this point Johnson utilizes the Berkeleyan idealism which he had adopted years before. "I know," he said, "that I am not the cause of any of those impressions that are made upon my senses; light, colors, sounds, tangible qualities, etc. . . . Nor can they be without a cause, nor yet from any senseless, inert, or unactive cause. . . . They must therefore be the constant effects of an intelligent cause, intimately present with me, and incessantly active upon me, who continually produceth all these sensations in my mind, correspondent to the archetypes in his all-comprehending intellect, according to certain stable, or fixed rules . . . which are commonly called the laws of nature. When therefore I consider the whole system of these sensible, as well as the intelligible, objects that surround me, and under the impression of which I continually live, I must conclude, that I live, and move, and have my being, in Him, who is the perpetual and Almighty Author of them" (II, 465).

These "sensible objects are all firmly connected together . . . so as to constitute one most beautiful whole, which we call the natural world." Furthermore, "they are all contrived in the best manner to render them subservient to all the purposes of my subsistence and well-being, and that of the whole rational and moral system, which we call the Moral World." From this it must be concluded that God is "not only an infinitely wise and powerful, but moreover an infinitely kind and benevolent Being" (II, 465).

In the second edition of this treatise Johnson inserted a paragraph in which he drew a specific parallel between the natural and moral worlds which he had suggested in the first edition. "For," he said, "as I see all the order, harmony and usefulness of nature depends on the laws of . . . attraction . . . and also on the surprising instincts by which the several tribes of animals are led to provide for their subsistence, and the continuance of their species, which can no otherwise be accounted for, than from the mere passive impressions of the great Almighty Mind . . . so I observe all the order, harmony and happiness of the moral world, depends on the laws of benevolence . . ., which strong tendency of benevolence in the moral world, is plainly analogous to attraction and instincts in the natural, and must accordingly be a like passive impression of the Parent-governing Mind, who plainly designs hereby to keep the moral world together, and in order." For this purpose "all created minds are passively enlightened, to have a quick sense, and intuitive evidence of the fit, the fair, and decent in behavior and thence, the laws by which this principle of benevolence must be regulated, in order to their universal harmony and happiness" (II, 468-469).

Such was the parallel which Johnson had in mind when, in the first edition, he dealt with the regulation of the moral world. "It cannot therefore be," he said, "that as he [God] evidently governs the natural world, in a passive manner, suitable to its passive nature, by the laws which He hath established to Himself . . . so he must much more govern the moral world . . . in a manner suitable to its rational and moral nature." Man can expect to be treated "as a reasonable and moral agent" and to be judged on the basis of his "use of the abilities and talents" which have been committed to his trust (II, 470). Being capable of making his own choices because of freedom of the will, man can misuse his gifts.

This misuse of our liberty, powers, and advantages is sin, which "consists in the voluntary opposition of our

117

wills to the known will of God, or the constitution which He hath made" (II, 472).

The question then arises, "Why hath God made me at all peccable, or capable of sin?" "This," Johnson said, "would be the same as to ask, why hath he made me capable of duty; or, why hath he made me a free agent? But this would be a strange question; for without liberty I should be destitute of one of the chief excellencies of my rational nature, and should not be capable of either duty or sin, properly speaking; for as sin consists in a free and voluntary disobedience, so duty consists in a free and willing obedience to the known will of God. So that without a power of liberty or free agency, there could have been no such thing as either virtue or vice, praise or blame; nor can either the one or the other obtain, but in proportion to the knowledge we have, or may have, of what we ought to do, and the powers we are furnished with, either to do or forbear" (II, 472).

Thus the government of the moral world, which includes both rewards and punishments, must, in order to meet the requirements of justice, allow a liberty, which, when abused, results in sin. This sin is, however, the fault of man, not of God, since the liberty which makes it possible was granted to man for his benefit and happiness.

Johnson's third question was, "For what end was I made and have my being?" This he answered in a chapter entitled "Of the End of our Being, and of our future State."

Again Johnson absolves God from guilt for the "mischief and misery which do, in the nature of things, necessarily result from sin and vice." It cannot be supposed, however, Johnson thought, that this misery would be God's "primary design," or that God would lay men "under a necessity of sinning, that they might be finally miserable; for this would, in effect, be absolutely to design their misery, and delight in it as such, which to Him must be infinitely impossible."

In accordance with his own conception of God's attributes, Johnson asserted: "On the contrary, since God is evidently a most kind and benevolent Being, and could therefore have no other than kind and benevolent ends, in giving being to His rational creatures, it is plain that His primary intention must have been so far from making them to be miserable, that He did undoubtedly make them with a design that they might be, in some good degree, happy, in the participation and enjoyment of His goodness, in proportion to their several capacities and qualifications" (II, 475).

Also, in accordance with his conception of man's qualities, he explained: "Inasmuch . . . as God hath made us to be intelligent, free, active creatures; and since our happiness must immediately depend upon the right use of these powers, and must consist in the free and vigorous use of them, in conformity to the great law of our nature, which is the inward sense of our own reason and consciences; it must accordingly be His design, not only that we should be happy, but that we should be so by means of our own activity, and by always freely acting reasonably, and consequently that we should cultivate and improve our reason in the best manner we can . . . in order to make a right judgment how we ought to affect and act, and conduct ourselves to the best advantage for our own happiness" (II, 476).

The conclusion of the speculative part of *A System of Morality* is "that the true and ultimate end of my being, can be nothing short of this; that I may be as happy as my condition will admit of here, and eternally and completely happy in the future state of my existence, in the enjoyment of God, and all that is good, and in the perfection of knowledge and virtue, which alone can render me capable thereof" (II, 483-484).

In Part II, THE PRACTICAL *Part of Moral* Philosophy, Johnson answers the last three of the six questions outlined in the main body of the book, proceeding "to deduce the duties that result from them" (II, 485).

The first of these questions is "what I ought to be? Or . . . what I ought to do, in order to answer the end of my being?" To answer this question, Johnson said, "I must . . . duly consider myself in all the relations in which I stand." "And they may all be reduced to these three general heads, *viz.*, to myself, my God, and my neighbor" (II, 485, 488).

The first of these Johnson treated in a chapter entitled "Of the Duties which we owe to ourselves." These duties Johnson called "Human Virtues" and considered them a necessary basis for the "divine virtues" and the "social virtues."

Basing his treatment of "Human Virtues" on the conceptions of human nature presented in the speculative part of the book, Johnson asserted: "From what hath been said, it is plain, that the first duty incumbent upon me, as a reasonable active creature, in order to answer the end of my being, is, to cultivate and improve the reason and understanding which God hath given me, to be the governing principle and great law of my nature, to search and know the truth, to find out wherein true happiness consists, and the means necessary to it, and from thence the measures of right and wrong, and to discipline and regulate my will, affections, appetites and passions, according to reason and truth, that I may freely and readily embrace the one and reject the other, in order that I may be truly happy" (II, 490).

Thus reason has two primary functions: to discover truth and to regulate the passions. Further, "our reason and consideration is manifestly given us to make a just estimate of things, and to preside over our inferior powers, and to proportion our several appetites and passions, to the real nature, and intrinsic value of their respective objects so as not to love or hate, hope or fear, joy or grieve, be pleased or displeased at any thing beyond the real importance of it to our happiness or misery . . . ; it must therefore be my duty to keep a due balance among them within their proper bounds, and to take care that they do not exceed or fall short of the real nature and measure of their several objects; and specially so as not to suffer them to tempt or hurry me on to trespass upon any of the duties that I owe to God or man'' (II, 491).

Regarding man's duties to God, Johnson stated this general proposition: "My second relation is to God, my Maker, Preserver and Governor, which obligeth me, in faithfulness to Him, as well as to myself, to behave myself suitably to the character of such a glorious Being as He is on whom I depend, that I may be happy in Him: and this is Divine Virtue, or virtue due to the deity'' (II, 489). In the second edition Johnson added that this virtue "may be expressed by the general term, piety.'' This means that we must submit ourselves to God's moral government, must have confidence in Him, must revere Him, must be as near like Him as possible in all our "tempers and deportment,'' and must worship him (pp. 493-496).

"My third relation is,'' Johnson said, "to my fellow creatures, and especially those of my own species, of the same rational, social and immortal nature with myself, which obligeth me, both in faithfulness to myself and others, to behave suitably to the social character, or in such a manner as is fit, decent and right towards such a system of beings as they are, that I may be happy in them, and they in me; and this is called Social Virtue, or virtue due to society." "And," Johnson added in the second edition, "may be expressed by the general term, benevolence" (II, 489). These social duties must be exercised "both in those lesser societies founded in nature, which are called families, and those larger societies founded in compact, whether tacit or explicit, called civil governments." They "terminate in that noblest of all social passions, the love of our country and our species, joined with an ardent zeal for every thing that concerns the public weal" (II, 501).

Johnson's last two questions were: "Whether I am what I ought to be? And if not, What I ought to do, as a means in order to be and do what I ought, and so in order finally to answer the end of my being?" These questions Johnson dealt with together in a chapter entitled "Of the Subordinate Duties, or Means for the more ready and faithful discharge of the Duties above explained" (II, 501).

The first means of making sure that one performs these Duties is the practice of daily self-examination. If remissness in performance is discovered, remorse should follow and remorse should be succeeded by repentance and reformation. Along with this should go a resolution to avoid future lapses from duty. One should watch for particular weaknesses in his own personal character and resolve to guard against them. Also one must continually bear in mind that "there are most tremendous punishments attending our disobedience" and "on the other hand most glorious rewards attending a course of obedience" (II, 502-507).

Ending his treatment of duties on a religious note, Johnson declared that one who has followed the practices he has recommended can say to himself: "I shall, at length, be so inured to the love and practice of every virtue, human, divine and social, in the perfection of which consists the highest happiness of my reasonable

122

and immortal nature, that I shall at length be prepared to quit this present stage, and to give a good account of myself to God, being in some good measure qualified for that perfect state of virtue and consummate happiness, which is to be expected in the future state of my existence" (II, 507).

In 1752, six years after the *System of Morality* was issued, Johnson published a more comprehensive work entitled *Elementa Philosophica: Containing chiefly, Noetica, Or Things relating to the Mind or Understanding: and Ethica, or Things relating to the Moral Behaviour.* This work was published by Benjamin Franklin in Philadelphia and was dedicated to George Berkeley. The "Ethica," which constitutes the second part of the *Elementa,* is a new edition of the *System of Morality,* amplified by the insertion of numerous passages of new material.

The new part, entitled "Noetica," is described as containing "the First Principles of Human Knowledge. Being a LOGIC, Including both METAPHYSICS, and DIALECTICS, or the Art of REASONING. With a brief Pathology, and an Account of the gradual Progress of the Human Mind, from the first Dawnings of Sense to the highest Perfection, both Intellectual and Moral, of which it is capable. To which is prefixed, A Short INTRODUCTION to the Study of the *Sciences*" (II, 359). Since Johnson presented the last and highest stage of "perfection" as moral, it seems certain that one of the main purposes of the "Noetica" was to lay a general philosophical foundation for the "Ethica" which followed. Since, however, the original *System of Morality* contained a considerable amount of philosophical background for ethics which was not eliminated in the second edition, there is a good deal of repetition and overlapping in the two parts of the combined work.

The *Elementa Philosophica* was specifically designed

as a textbook for young students, and it contains not only material for educational use but also what may be considered as a philosophy of education.

In explaining his intention, Johnson said: "As I am of the opinion, that little manuals of the sciences, if they could be well done, would be of good use to young beginners; what I aim at in this little tract, is to be as useful to them as I can, in the studies of Metaphysics and Logics, and this in order to the more particular studies of nature and morals, by giving as clear definitions as I am able in few words, of the principal matters and terms whereof those studies consist; which I have endeavored to do, in an order of thoughts, gradually arising one after another, in a manner as instructive as could well be. . . . I have also proposed to show how these, taking their rise from the first beginnings of sense, proceed on through the other studies, to raise the mind to its highest perfection and happiness" (II, 360).

Johnson had utilized Berkeleyan idealism in the treatise on ethics and did so again in the "Noetica." "Tho' I would not be too much attached to any one author or system, exclusive of any others," he said, "yet whoever is versed in the writings of Bishop Berkeley, will be sensible that I am in a particular manner beholden to that excellent philosopher for several thoughts that occur in the following tract." In explanation of a particular feature of the present work, Johnson said: "And I was the rather willing to publish this logic, because I think metaphysics a necessary part of that science, and I apprehend it a great damage to the sciences that the old metaphysics are so much neglected, and that they might be rendered the more pleasant and useful by joining with them some improvements of the moderns" (II, 360).

The nature and purpose of the following introductory chapter was to present "a short general view of the whole system of learning, wherein young students may at once behold, as it were in miniature, the objects, boundaries, ends and uses of each of the sciences; their foundation in the nature of things; the natural order in which they lie, and their several relations and connections, both with respect to one another, and to the general end, *viz.,* our hapiness, pursued thro' them all" (II, 360).

In the chapter thus promised, Johnson not only provided what he considered a logically organized outline of the fields of learning but also dealt with the order in which the subjects are to be used in the educational process.

He had defined ethics as "the art of living happily." His conception of knowledge in general is similar. "Learning," he said, ". . . implies the knowledge of every thing useful to our well-being and true happiness in this life, or our supreme happiness in the life to come."

His survey of the fields of knowledge aimed to reduce "all the various parts of learning to these two, philology, or the study of words and other signs, and philosophy, or the study of the things signified by them" (II, 361).

Philology not only stands first in Johnson's classification of the fields of learning but it is the subject which should be studied first, since "the understanding of young persons, for the fifteen or sixteen years of their life are not ripe enough to enter into th sublimer studies of philosophy." Young people "must be early initiated into the rudiments of grammar . . . both in their mother tongue, and other languages, especially the French, Latin, Greek and Hebrew." "And as soon as they have got a good notion of pure speech by the study of grammar, let them learn the nature of figurative speech in rhetoric." They should then study the chief literary forms: oratory, history, and poetry. Along with poetry they are to learn literary criticism.

At the time when languages and the language arts are being studied elementary mathematics, which also belongs "to the doctrine of signs," should be pursued.

Johnson's second major division of the world of sciences, philosophy, or the study of the things signified by words, he proceeds to divide into two sub-divisions: (1) "General or common to all kinds of beings," and (2) "Special or peculiar to each kind of beings."

After students have made considerable progress in languages, they "proceed, secondly, to the further improvement of their understandings and active powers, in the sublimer studies of philosophy, which is the study of truth and wisdom, or the knowledge of things, as being what they really are, together with a conduct correspondent thereto, in the pursuit of true happiness; to which they must go on when they are sixteen or seventeen years old" (II, 363-364).

In order of educational use as well as of logical organization, the general subjects precede the special. These general subjects, which are "common to all kinds of beings," are logic and mathematics.

In order to "regulate both our tempers and manners" we must have "knowledge of God and ourselves" and for this purpose we must "be able to form to ourselves clear ideas and conceptions of those beings and things which we contemplate, whether bodies or spirits" (II, 364). To accomplish this, "Logic, or the art of reasoning, is very requisite." The foundation of logic is metaphysics, "which by some hath been called ontology, and is the noblest and most elevated part of science." Metaphysics "begins with sensible objects, and from them takes its rise to things purely intellectual, and treats of being, abstracted from every particular nature, whether body or spirit, and of all the general distinctions, connections and relations of things, whether sensible or intellectual, and so lays a foundation for clear and just reasoning, while we proceed upon stable and unerring principles" (II, 364-365).

Based on this metaphysical foundation, "logic teacheth us the rules of thinking regularly, and reasoning justly, whereby we learn to distinguish truth from falsehood, and proceed from things simple to things compound, and from things precarious and contingent to things necessary, stable and eternal, which therefore will result in the clearest and justest views, both of all other things, and of the adorable excellencies of the divine nature, that our little minds are capable of" (II, 365).

After the basic principles of mathematics and logic have been learned, "we proceed to the application of them, first in the study of quantity in general, whether number or magnitude, in the sublimer mathematics." This includes algebra, plane and solid geometry, trigonometry, conic sections, and calculus. This enables us "to proceed with greater advantage in the study of nature" and "without it we cannot read with understanding the best things that have been written on that subject." Furthermore, "This sort of study hath likewise a direct tendency to lead us to an admiring sense of the Deity, in whose infinite treasures of eternal truth, we behold these connections and demonstrations, who hath made all things in number, measure and weight" (II, 365).

After the general subjects which apply to "all kinds of beings" come those which are "special or peculiar to each kind of beings." "From the contemplation of quantity in the abstract," Johnson said, "we go on next to the consideration of it in the concrete, or in the objects of sense . . . in the endlessly various bodies that compose this mighty frame of heaven and earth, and the principles and laws of motion . . . which are the subjects of

127

physics or natural philosophy: the foundation of which is mechanics." Then we proceed in "geology . . . to contemplate this globe of earth, in all its parts and furniture; the elements, fire, air, water and earth; the stones, mines, minerals, meteors, plants, and animals, and particularly the wonderful structure of our own bodies."

After studying the earth and the things pertaining to it "we launch forth into the vast and unmeasurable ether, and in astronomy we contemplate the heavens and stars . . . and particularly our sun, with his splendid chorus of planets and comets . . . and the laws of their motions." From contemplating this "amazing scene, in which nature displays her surprising phenomena, and invites us to . . . trace out infinite wisdom, power and goodness . . . we are led to behold, acknowledge, admire and adore the great author of all things" (II, 366).

"And this prepares us," Johnson said, "to proceed a step higher, and from the sensible or natural world, to go on to the contemplation of the intelligent or moral world; from the world of bodies, to the world of spirits, which, . . . being intelligent and moral agents, are the great subject of ethics, or moral philosophy." The foundation for this is a study of "our own souls, their powers and operations, both perceptive and active." From this we proceed to "the more particular contemplation of the Deity . . ., which is called theology." Knowledge of ourselves and of God provides the basis for ethics, or "the art of living happily by the universal practice of virtue."

The treatise which follows this introduction is virtually all devoted to a study of the human mind and its activities. "By the human mind," Johnson said, "we mean that principle of sense, intelligence and free activity, which we feel within ourselves, or rather feel ourselves to be furnished with those objects and powers, and under those confinements and limitations, under which it hath pleased our great Creator to place us in this present state" (II, 373).

Since, in this present state, we are "minds connected with . . . bodies," "our minds perceive and act by means of our bodily organs." "The immediate object of . . . our perceptions and actions we call ideas." An "idea" is "any immediate object of the mind in thinking, whether sensible or intellectual" (II, 373). Since we are born without any ideas in our minds, all knowledge is derived from "sense and consciousness."

By sense we mean, "those perceptions we have of objects *ab extra,* or by means of the several organs of our bodies." In accounting for these perceptions, Johnson used Berkeleyan idealism. According to this view, the sensations or ideas in our minds are the real things. Johnson preferred this view rather than the theory that sensations are pictures "of things without us," because these pictures might be supposed to be inaccurate and therefore we might be led into skepticism about the validity of any knowledge (II, 375).

Besides these perceptions of objects *ab extra,* we have consciousness, or "our perception of objects *ab intra,* or from reflecting or turning the eye of the mind inward and observing what passeth within itself." Furthermore we have imagination and memory.

We are also conscious of having, in addition to perception and imagination, something which can be called "pure intellect." This is a "power of conceiving of abstracted or spiritual objects, and the relations between our several ideas and conceptions, and the various dispositions, exertions and actions of our minds, and the complex notions resulting from all these." By this power we form "notions or conceptions."

Johnson then gave a list of these "intellectual and active powers:"

129

"1. The simple apprehension of objects, and their several relations, connections and dependencies, arising from our comparing our ideas and conceptions one with another.

"2. Judging of true or false, according as things appear to agree or disagree, to be connected or not connected one with another.

"3. Reasoning or inferring one thing from another, and methodizing them according to their connections and order" (II, 378).

These are, Johnson said, "the subject of logics" and to each of these operations of the mind he devoted a chapter. Of these chapters the most technical is the one dealing with "reasoning or inferring one thing from another," in which he described the different kinds of syllogisms.

The human mind includes other activities besides the intellectual with reference to things presented to it, for besides the intellectual processes described by logic we also have within us an "intellectual light" which is derived from the "universal presence and action of the Deity" (II, 379). Because of this "intellectual light," we have an "intuitive sense of true and false, good and bad, right and wrong" (II, 425). "And," Johnson said, "from this intuitive intellectual light it is (as I conceive) that we derive what we call taste and judgment, and with respect to morals, what some call the moral sense or the conscience, which are only a sort of quick intuitive sense or apprehension of the decent and amiable, of beauty and deformity, of true and false, and of right and wrong, or duty and sin." "And it is," he declared, "the chief business of culture, art and instruction, to awaken and turn our attention to it, and assist us in making deductions from it" (II, 380).

Since Johnson was treating logic, not as a self-contained subject, but as based on metaphysics and providing a basis for ethics, he followed his account of the operations of the intellect with a chapter entitled "Of the Mind affecting, willing and acting." "Having . . . given some account of the subject of logics, which relate to the conduct of the intellect in its exertions," he said, "I now go on to give a short sketch of the subject of ethics, which relate to our conduct of our affections and behavior" (II, 417).

A brief outline of the non-intellectual activities of the mind which are to be considered in the study of ethics followed:

"1. Of our affecting or disaffecting things, according as they appear good or bad.

"2. Of our choosing or refusing, willing, or nilling them, according as we affect or disaffect them.

"3. Of our freely acting, or forbearing to act, according to the judgment and choice we have made."

"First we are to consider the affections or passions . . . , the doctrine or explication of which is called pathology." "Now, by the passions," he said, "we mean in general, such affections or disaffections, inclinations or aversions, as we experience in ourselves, upon feeling or expecting that pleasure or uneasiness with which any object is attended" (II, 418).

"These passions are natural to us, and, as such, must be considered as part of the frame of our natures, and consequently as being implanted in us by the Author of our nature, for answering very wise and good ends, relating to our happiness, and therefore are so far from being evil in themselves, that they have the nature of good, as well as all our other faculties, and so, like the rest, become morally good or evil according to the use we make of them." Regarding the general function of the passions, Johnson said that "they are, as it were, the wings of the soul, by which it is carried on with vehemence and impetuosity in its several pursuits; and, as

131

it were, its springs, by which it is animated and invigorated in all its exertions" (II, 419). The passions, however, must be regulated. "And for this purpose were we furnished with the powers of reason and conscience, that they might preside over the passions, and make a right judgment of their several objects . . . and restrain them from all exhorbitancies and irregularities . . ." Johnson concluded therefore that "one of the chief concerns in culture and education is, to discipline and moderate the passions, and to inure them to a ready submission to the dictates of reason and conscience" (II, 420).

Johnson treated together the last two topics in his outline, i.e., (1) the power of choosing one thing and refusing the other, and (2) the power of free activity, whereby we are able spontaneously to exert ourselves for obtaining the one, and avoiding the other.

In choosing and refusing, both the reason and the will are involved, since our "reason was . . . given us to enable us to make a right judgment what we ought to choose and avoid, and to do and forbear . . . ; and our will consists in freely resolving and determining ourselves to the one or the other, as they shall appear to the judgment."

The power to choose or reject, and to act or refrain from acting implies freedom. "For," Johnson said, "freedom or liberty consisteth in having a power to act, or not to act, as we please, and consequently to suspend judging or acting, till we have taken opportunity to make as deliberate and exact a judgment as ever we can, what is best for us in the whole, to do or forbear." "Necessity, on the other hand, considered as opposed to liberty, implieth, that it is out of our power to suspend acting, or to do otherwise than we do, in which case there can be neither praise nor blame" (II, 421).

So far Johnson had been describing the activities, both

intellectual and emotional, of the mature mind. Since this was an educational work, however, he added a chapter entitled "Of the Progress of the mind, from its first Notices, towards its utmost Perfection."

Beginning with an account of what children can learn by means of the senses and by observation before they learn to read, Johnson proceeded to outline a plan of education. This is a recapitulation of the survey of the arts and sciences which he had already given in an introductory chapter, with special emphasis of the effect of these studies on the growing mind.

Presuming that, by means of these studies and by observation, the mind of the young person had been "convinced of the existence of the Deity," Johnson said that "now it must be led on further, in moral philosophy, theology, ethics, &c. to the contemplation of Him, and that world of spirits derived from Him . . ." (II, 432).

Thus Johnson had, by his presentation of metaphysics, logic, and a general outline of knowledge, laid a foundation for the study of ethics. Hence this first part of the *Elementa Philosophica* provides a preparation for the revised edition of the *System of Morality* which follows. The *Elementa*, which was written as an educational work, was actually used as a textbook at the Academy of Philadelphia and at King's College, established in 1755 with Johnson as its first president.

Except for the statement in the preface to the *System of Morality* that, on account of the prevalence of Antinomianism and skepticism, a defense of morality was needed, there is nothing in the *Elementa* which is specifically related to the times. It seems probable, however, since he was a churchman as well as a philosopher, that he hoped that his book might serve the cause of religion in New England. About the state of religion at the time he was somewhat disturbed. In a report to the Society for the Propagation of the Gospel, written in 1750, in pleading for the establishment of an American Episcopate he observed "that our dissenting brethren are really their own greatest enemies as well as ours, in opposing bishops being sent into the country, for their case is very deplorable among themselves since the late enthusiasm hath thrown them into so many feuds, contentions, and separations, which the awe of a bishop would we believe tend much to abate." He also said that "the very cause of Christianity in general suffers and will suffer more and more extremely, to the great advantage of infidelity, for want of some great and worthy person in such a superior station to stem the torrent" (III, 242).

In 1753, a year after the publication of the *Elementa,* Johnson reported to the Society for the Propagation of the Gospel: "As the late enthusiasm is much abated, free thinking as it is called which is worse, takes place of it, and now Chubb, Tindal, and the *Independent Whig* grow much in vogue, who do more mischief than the others, so that we have now these fatal principles to oppose and guard against" (III, 247).

Johnson had originally accepted Berkeley's idealism partly because he thought that it was the answer to deism. Now, at a time when deism was menacing religion in New England, he may have felt that his book, although not polemical, could provide some protection of Christianity against the "torrent" of infidelity. What the actual effect of his book was cannot be known. He used some of his philosophical ideas in simplified form, however, in sermons preached to his own and other congregations, and they therefore reached a wider audience than his book alone could have done. The book itself made a favorable impression on at least one reader. Thomas Secker, Bishop of Oxford told Johnson in a letter that he had "explained and recommended just reasoning, virtue, and religion, so as not only to make them well understood but ardently loved'' (II, 331).

V

JONATHAN EDWARDS VS. ARMINIANISM

Not long after the publication of *A Treatise Concerning Religious Affections* (1746), Jonathan Edwards became alarmed about the spread of Arminianism and determined to combat it.

At the time when he made this decision and began making preparations for his attack, a controversy which followed the publication of Johnson's *Letter from Aristides to Authades* and the sermons of Beach and Caner had begun.

Johnson, when he published the *Letter,* had anticipated that he would be accused of Arminianism. This expectation was fulfilled in Jonathan Dickinson's *Vindication of God's Sovereign Free Grace* (1746), in which the Calvinistic conception of sovereignty was asserted and Johnson and Beach were declared to be Arminians.

It was at this time that Edwards determined to make a further study of Arminianism. From a letter to his former pupil and disciple, Joseph Bellamy, dated January 15, 1747, it is known that he had read Johnson's *Letter* and Dickinson's *Vindication.* In his letter to Bellamy, Edwards also included the following request: "If you could Enquire of Dr. Johnson or Mr. Beach or some other what is the best Book on the Arminian side, for their defense of their notion of Free will; and whether there be any better and more full than Whitby, I should be glad . . . ''[1]

---

[1] *New England Quarterly,* I, 231.

135

While Edwards proceeded with his plan to prepare his attack on Arminianism, the controversy between the Anglicans and the Calvinists continued. John Beach replied to Dickinson's *Vindication* in a pamphlet entitled *God's Sovereignty and His Universal Love to the Souls of Men Reconciled* (1747), which strongly reasserted the idea that freedom of the will is a necessary condition of responsible moral agency. Johnson also answered Dickinson in *A Letter ... in Defense of Aristocles to Authades* (1747), in which he argued that the Calvinistic doctrine of predestination is almost identical with the mechanistic determinism, or doctrine of necessity, of some of the Deists. Of this doctrine, Johnson said to Dickinson, "And I can't but observe to you here, that there can scarcely be a more mischievous doctrine advanced among mankind than this necessitating doctrine of yours; for it tends at once to destroy all religion and morality, and all civil and family government, and render them unmeaning and ridiculous things; for what signify all laws and rules of action, all motives taken from praise or blame, hope or fear, reward and punishment, while every thing we do is under a fatal necessity, and we can do no otherwise than we do" (III, 200).

Johnson's *Letter from Aristocles to Authades* was also attacked in a lengthy pamphlet entitled *A Vindication of Gospel-Truth, and Refutation of Some Dangerous Errors* (1747), by Jedediah Mills. This was actually a defense of Calvinistic doctrines and an attack on the views of Johnson which Mills considered to be "common to those in the *Arminian Scheme*" (p. 57). Mills wrote this pamphlet not merely as a reply to Johnson, but also, he said, "with an aim ... to prevent, at least in some Measure, an Inundation of (what are commonly called) *Pelagian* and *Arminian* Errors; which to my best Observation, have a very threatening Aspect on the dear Churches of God in this Land, and do speak their Danger of being sooner or later carried off, at least in some essential Points from the *Gospel of Christ* (which our Fathers valued above all their wordly Interests, and which they brought over into this Wilderness, and left as a precious Legacy to their Posterity) even to the receiving another Gospel" (pp. vii-viii).

One of the main themes of Johnson's *Letter from Aristocles to Authades* was that the Bible contains many promises of reward to those who perform their duties and that God is under obligation to fulfill these promises. Mills argued that God offered encouragements but not promises of certain reward for effort, and that an obligation to reward effort would place limitations on God's absolute sovereignty (p. 15).

According to Mills, Johnson's doctrine meant that God's promises were extended to all, including the unregenerate. "This supposes," he said, "some acceptable degree of *moral Goodness, intrinsick Worth,* or *true Excellency,* in these *Doings* of the Unregenerate; something in them of vital and true *Holiness,* in God's Account: and implies that his Method of *saving us is by Works of Righteousness, which we have done,* and not meerly *according to his Mercy,* or sovereign Grace" (p. 39).

Meanwhile Edwards had already formulated the plan for his attack on Arminianism. In a letter written in the summer of 1747 to John Erskine, a minister of the Church of Scotland, he said: "I have thought of writing something particularly and largely on the Arminian controversy, in distinct discourses on the various points in dispute, to be published successively, beginning first with a discourse concerning the Freedom of the Will, and Moral Agency; endeavouring fully and thoroughly to state and discuss those points of Liberty and Necessity, Moral and Physical Inability, Efficacious Grace, and the ground of virtue and vice, reward and punishment, blame and praise, with regard to the dispositions and actions of reasonable creatures.''

The controversy between the Anglicans and the Calvinistic Congregationalists was not yet concluded, however. In reply to Beach's *God's Sovereignty*, Jonathan Dickinson was beginning the composition of *A Second Vindication of God's Sovereign Free Grace*. He died, however, before the work was finished, and it was completed by his brother Moses in 1748. In this *Second Vindication*, Jonathan Dickinson accused Beach of Pelagianism, and declared that his Arminian interpretation of the articles of the Church of England was something that ''was never once heard of'' at the time when they were formulated (pp. 31-35, and 45). Moses Dickinson charged Johnson with holding unsound views regarding original sin.

This argument was terminated in 1748 with an answer to the Dickinsons entitled *A Second Vindication of God's Free Grace Indeed* by John Beach, with a preface by Johnson. In this preface Johnson, in answer to Jonathan Dickinson, defended the doctrine of free-will against the doctrine of necessity, defended his view of original sin against Moses Dickinson's accusation, and replied briefly to Jedediah Mills' attack on him.

Mills, as we have seen, had objected to Johnson's idea that God has made promises of reward to men for their performance of duties. This objection, Johnson said, was the result of the misunderstanding of certain Biblical texts. ''And,'' he said, ''this misunderstanding of these . . . texts . . . appears to me to be owing to the want of just criticism.'' It was also due, he thought, ''to that old scholastical philosophy of the Roman Catholics, which perverted the plainness and simplicity of the Gospel, being a system of many centuries later than the Gospel itself, and was not at once purged away by the Reformation'' (III, 213).

In this series of disputes between Anglicans and Calvinists several theological doctrines had been argued. The
most important point on which the parties differed, however, was the doctrine of free will.

Just after the Anglican-Calvinist controversy was concluded, another quarrel began, this time between members of the Congregational clergy. Here the chief topic
of contention was the position of good works in the
scheme of justification.

In 1748 Robert Breck, of Springfield, described the
problem posed to ministers by the respective claims of
works and faith. "Is it," he said, "the duty of the Ministers of the Gospel frequently to urge upon Believers
a Care to maintain good Works, then certainly they
ought not to be reproach'd for doing it; And yet, I verily
believe this has often been the case, in this Land, of
late Years." Breck admitted that "if we neglect to
preach up Faith, this is also a just matter of Reproach."
"But if we insist upon the Necessity of a holy Life,
proceeding from Gospel-Motives, why should we be
blam'd ... And yet, I believe many Ministers have been
reproach'd and vilified, have been called legal Preachers,
Arminians, &c., for no other Reason, but only because
they have conscientiously ... press'd upon them that
believ'd, a Care to maintain good Works."

In the years immediately preceding Breck's remarks,
there had been no published writings containing the kind
of accusations he complained about. These accusations
were undoubtedly expressed, however, in conversation
and perhaps in unpublished sermons.

But within the year (1749) a quarrel, both acrimoni-
ous and extensive, broke out following a sermon preached
in 1749 by Lemuel Briant, of Braintree, Massachusetts,
entitled *The Absurdity and Blasphemy of Depretiating
Moral Virtue,* based on the text: "All our righteous-
nesses are as filthy rags." This text had been cherished

by Calvinists because it was supposed to support the doctrine that there is no real merit in any of the deeds of the unregenerate. Briant, however, held that the text was meant to apply, not to men in general, but only to the state of morals among the Hebrews at the time of Isaiah. He maintained that all sincere men are capable of righteousness and that the inculcation of morality is the most important theme in Scripture. The traditional interpretation of his text was, he thought, but one of many erroneous interpretations of Scriptural texts produced in times of ignorance and superstition. In illustrating this point, he incidentally repudiated the Calvinistic doctrines of election and irresistible grace.

This sermon was followed by nine publications in which Briant was attacked and defended. The first of the replies was a sermon entitled *The Absurdity and Blasphemy of Substituting the Personal Righteousness of Men in the Room of the Surety-Righteousness of Christ,* by John Porter of Bridgewater, Connecticut.

Alarmed by the prevalence of such doctrines as Briant's, Porter exclaimed, "Alas! Alas! that there are so many professed Preachers of Righteousness of the younger Sort." After having argued that reliance on personal righteousness for justification is dangerous because it builds up a false sense of security, Porter asserted, "From what has been said we may learn, that the *good old Calvinistical Way* of preaching up Justification by Faith in the Righteousness of Christ, has by far a greater Tendency to promote *true Gospel Obedience,* than the *modern Arminian Way*" (p. 22).

To this sermon was appended an attestation signed by five ministers who expressed their hope "that this *seasonable Discourse* will be a Means . . . of establishing many in the Truth . . . as it hath been taught in *these Churches from the beginning of New-England.*" "And," they added, "we cannot but lament the dreadful Increase of Arminian and other *Errors* in the Land, among Ministers and People'' (p. 31).

Briant himself, in a reply to Porter and other critics, also took note of a change that had taken place—a change, as he saw it, for the better. Speaking of himself and his congregation, he said that ''we are desirous to know the Truth.'' And with reference to his congregation in particular, that '' 'tis the Disposition of my Charge to seek for it in the holy Scripture without any slavish attachment to humane Schemes.'' As to the growth of a tolerant spirit, he observed that ''the Perils, that in Times of Ignorance and implicit believing have attended Freedom and Plainness of Speech, . . . are very considerably abated.''

In view of the disposition of Briant's congregation it is not surprising that he received their support when, in 1753, an ecclesiastical council condemned both his conduct and his doctrine. A committee composed of members of his Church not only cleared him of all charges but approved his doctrines and commended his attitude.

At the time of the controversy over Briant, John Bass, of Ashford, Connecticut, was also accused of Arminianism. According to his own statement, Bass denied the Calvinistic doctrines of election and limited atonement. As to the doctrine of original sin, he believed that men had had to suffer because of Adam's sin, but were not to incur any other punishment on account of it. Upon complaint from his congregation about his doctrine, Bass was investigated by the Consociation of Windham County and dismissed from his pastorate in 1751. The case of Bass, like that of Briant, brought forth further complaints about the spread of unsound doctrine. In a book attacking both Briant and Bass, Samuel Niles, of Braintree, warned that it was necessary for orthodox ministers to be on their guard, ''Especially as these *Churches* appear now, more than ever, in danger of being corrupted

141

by *Arminian Errors, or worse* . . . propagated by several . . . lately introduced into the *Pastoral Charge.*" Then, explaining why it had become necessary for orthodox ministers to describe the doctrines of the New England churches as "Calvinistical," he said that "this Note of Distinction has but lately arose among us, occasioned very much by the late Growth and Discovery of *Arminianism,* which has now made it's open and formidable Appearance in some of our Churches."

Such was the situation in the Congregational Churches of New England in the early 1750's. Meanwhile Edwards' promised book against Arminianism was still in the making, because of serious interruptions in his work. In 1748, David Brainerd, fiancé of one of Edwards' daughters and a young man of exemplary piety, died, and Edwards felt impelled to write and publish his biography. Then, in 1749, began a controversy between Edwards and his parishioners regarding qualifications for full membership in the church, or the right to participate in communion services. This problem had arisen because Edwards' grandfather, Solomon Stoddard, his predecessor in the pulpit at Northampton, had opened the communion to all respectable people in the parish as he considered it to be a converting ordinance. This was a departure from the traditional New England custom of admitting to communion only those who were judged to be converted. Edwards attempted to restore this restriction, and in support of his position published *An Humble Inquiry into the Rules . . . concerning the Qualifications Requisite to a Complete Standing and Full Communion with the Visible Church* (1749). As a result of bitter opposition to his proposal among his parishioners, he was, in accordance with the recommendation of a church council, dismissed from his pastorate in 1750.

In his *Farewell Sermon,* preached in July, 1750, Edwards, after giving the congregation advice and warning on various points, warned: "Another thing that vastly concerns the future prosperity of the town, is, that you should watch against the encroachment of Error; and particularly *Arminianism,* and doctrines of like tendency." Alluding to the time when there had been a "Great noise . . . in this Part of the Countrey about Arminianism" on account of the dispute over the ordination of Robert Breck, Edwards continued: "You were many of you, as I well remember, much alarmed, with the apprehension of the danger of these corrupt principles, near sixteen years ago. But the danger then was small, in comparison with what it appears now: these doctrines, at this day, are much more prevalent, than they were then." Edwards apparently thought that the recent spread of Arminian principles had begun in the midst of the Great Awakening. "The progress they have made, within this seven years," he said, "seems to have been vastly greater than at any time in the like period." "And they are still prevailing, and creeping into almost all parts of the land." Then, with reference to his own congregation, he said: "And I have of late perceived some things among yourselves, that show that you are far from being out of danger, but on the contrary remarkably exposed. The elder people may perhaps think themselves sufficiently fortified against infection . . . But let the case of the elder people be as it will, the rising generations are doubtless greatly exposed. These principles are exceedingly taking with corrupt nature and are what young people . . . are easily led away with."

Then, in a warning which included a reference to what had happened in Boston, Edwards said: "And if these principles should greatly prevail in this town, as they very lately have done in another large town I could name, formerly greatly noted for religion, and so for a long time, it will threaten the spiritual and eternal ruin of

143

this people, in the present and future generation. Therefore you have need of the greatest and most diligent care and watchfulness with respect to this matter."

In 1751 Edwards moved to Stockbridge, where he was pastor of the local church and missionary to the Indians. Although he was now free from involvement with affairs of Northampton, he was not even yet able to complete his book on the will. His treatise on qualifications for church membership had been attacked in a pamphlet by Solomon Williams, and to this he replied in *Misrepresentations Corrected, and Truth Vindicated,* published in 1752.

His plan for the book on the will was now, however, quite fully formulated. In a letter to John Erskine, dated July 7, 1752, he said: "I hope now, in a short time to be at leisure to resume my design, of writing something on the Arminian controversy. I have no thought of going through with all parts of the controversy at once; but the subject, which I intended, God willing, first to write something upon, was *Freewill and Moral Agency;* endeavouring, with as much exactness as I am able, to consider the nature of that freedom of moral agents, which makes them the proper subjects of moral government, moral precepts, . . . praise and blame, rewards and punishments: strictly examining the modern notions of these things, endeavouring to demonstrate their most palpable inconsistency and absurdity; endeavouring also to bring the late great objections and outcries against Calvinistic divinity . . . to the test of the strictest reasoning, and especially and particularly that great objection, in which the modern writers have so much gloried, so long triumphed . . . viz. That the Calvinistic notions of God's moral government are contrary to the common sense of mankind."

Although Edwards was impelled to write his book by his fear of the growth of Arminianism in New England, he did not attack any of the New England Arminians, either Anglican or Congregational. Instead, he chose to refute the views of weightier English writers who had dealt with the subject with which he was concerned. In his letter to Erskine, he said that he proposed "to take particular notice of the writings of Dr. Whitby, and Mr. Chubb, and the writings of some others, who, though not properly Pelagians, nor Arminians, yet, in their notions of the freedom of the will, have, in the main, gone into the same scheme." Among these "others," the most important was Isaac Watts.

Of these three writers, Thomas Chubb was an Arian, who later became a moderate Deist; Watts was a moderate Calvinist, who had written a book in support of the doctrine of free-will; and Daniel Whitby was an Anglican Arminian. It was Whitby who represented most fully the theological point of view which Edwards was combatting.

In 1710 Whitby had published a large book with an excessively long title which Edwards conveniently abbreviated to read *Discourse on the Five Points*. In this work Whitby refuted each of the Calvinistic doctrines as they had been formulated by the Synod of Dort in 1619. An important part of his procedure was to demonstrate that these doctrines had not appeared in theology before the time of St. Augustine and were therefore not a part of the original body of Christian beliefs. If they were true, he thought, it would be unjust to punish men for actions which, on account of depravity, election, etc., they cannot avoid and for which they cannot be held personally responsible. Also, Whitby thought, if men are to be held responsible and are to be subject to blame and punishment. they must be capable of making their own choices by free acts of the will.

Edwards' book was finally completed about the middle of 1753 and published early in 1754. The intention and scope of the work, which had been explained in the letters to Erskine, are clearly indicated by the full title: *A Careful and Strict Enquiry into the Modern Prevailing Notions of that Freedom of Will, Which Is Supposed to Be Essential to Moral Agency, Vertue and Vice, Reward and Punishment, Praise and Blame.* It is thus not merely a technical philosophical study of the will as such but also a study of the will in relation to moral responsibility.

In explaining the importance of his subject Edwards said:

"Of all kinds of knowledge that we can ever obtain, the knowledge of God, and the knowledge of ourselves, are the most important. As religion is the great business, for which we are created, and on which our happiness depends; and as religion consists in an intercourse between ourselves and our Maker; and so has its foundation in God's nature and in ours, and in the relation that God and we stand in to each other; therefore a true knowledge of both must be needful in order to true religion. But the knowledge of ourselves consists chiefly in right apprehensions concerning those two faculties of our nature, the *understanding* and the *will*. Both are very important: yet the science of the latter must be confessed to be of greatest moment; inasmuch as all virtue and religion have their seat more immediately in the will, consisting more especially in right acts and habits of ths faculty. And the grand question about the freedom of the will, is the main point that belongs to the science of the will."[2]

Edwards had previously dealt briefly with the will in connection with the affections, which he took to be only unusually lively exercises of this faculty. Now he treated the will without any consideration of the affections.

---

[2] *Freedom of the Will*, ed. Paul Ramsay (Yale University Press, 1957), p. 133. Subsequent references are to this edition.

146

He defined the will as "that faculty or power or principle of mind by which it is capable of choosing: an act of the will is an act of choosing or choice" (p. 137).

He then stated some ideas about what lies behind these acts of choosing which are basic to his later argument. "By 'determining the will,'" he said, ". . . must be intended, causing that the act of will or choice should be thus, and not otherwise: and the will is said to be determined, when, in consequence of some action, or influence its choice is directed to, and fixed upon a particular object. . . . To talk of determination of the will, supposes an effect, which must have a cause." It is the use of this principle of causation that is a distinguishing feature of Edwards' treatise.

"If," he continued, "the will be determined, there is a determiner." If those are right who say that the will determines itself, then it is both determiner and determined; "it is a cause that acts and produces effects upon itself, and is the object of its own influence and action" (p. 141).

Then, stating the cause of acts of the will, Edwards said that "it is that motive, which, as it stands in the view of the mind, is the strongest, that determines the will" (p. 141). A motive "must be something that is extant in the view or apprehension of the understanding, or perceiving faculty." Anything which is to be considered as "a motive to volition, or choice, is considered or viewed *as good*," that is, as "agreeable" or "pleasing to the mind" (p. 143). Edwards said that he preferred to say "that the will always *is* as the greatest apparent good, or as what appears most agreeable, is," rather "than to say that the will is *determined* by the greatest apparent good" (p. 144).

It is, however, not merely the object in itself that incites volition, but "the . . . act of volition itself is always determined by that in or about the mind's view of the object, which causes it to appear most agreeable." What causes an "object in view" to seem agreeable "is not only what appears in the object viewed, but also in the manner of the view, and the state and circumstances of the mind that views" (p. 144). In further explaining what he meant by "the state of mind" Edwards named "the particular temper which the mind has by nature, or that has been introduced and established by education, example, custom, or some other means; or the frame or state that the mind is in on a particular occasion" (pp. 146-147). "The choice of the mind never departs from that which, at that time, and with respect to the direct and immediate objects of that decision of the mind, appears most agreeable, all things considered" (p. 147).

Since the choices which are made are inevitable, Edwards introduces the term "necessity" in accounting for them. As he explained this concept, "Philosophical necessity is really nothing else than the full and fixed connection between the things signified by the subject and predicate of a proposition, which affirms something to be true" (p. 152).

For men there are two kinds of necessity: natural and moral. "By 'natural necessity' . . . I mean such necessity as men are under through the force of natural causes; as distinguished from what are called moral causes, such as habits and dispositions of the heart, and moral motives and inducements." "Moral necessity may be as absolute, as natural necessity. That is, the effect may be as perfectly connected with its moral cause, as a naturally necessary effect is with its natural cause." At least "in some cases, a previous bias and inclination, or the motive presented, may be so powerful, that the act of the will may be certainly and indissolubly connected therewith" (p. 157).

"What has been said of natural and moral necessity,"

Edwards continued, "may serve to explain natural and moral inability." A man may be able to do a certain thing even if he wills to do it because of physical or intellectual limitations in himself or because of external obstacles. This is *natural* inability. *"Moral inability* consists ... either in the want of inclination; or the strength of a contrary inclination; or the want of sufficient motives in view, to induce and excite the act of the will, or the strength of apparent motives to the contrary" (p. 159).

Thus, having shown that acts of the will are due to causes, both external objects and internal states of mind, Edwards was ready to discuss specifically the question of freedom of the will. Freedom he defined as the "power, opportunity, or advantage, that anyone has, to do as he pleases." Or in other words, "his being free from hindrance or impediment in the way of doing . . . as he wills." This power of doing what one wills can only belong to something that has a will. And "the will itself is not an agent that has a will: the power of choosing, itself, has not a power of choosing. That which has the power of volition or choice is the man or the soul, and not the power of volition itself" (p. 163). "Let the person come by his volition or choice how he will, yet, if he is able, and there is nothing in the way to hinder his pursuing and executing his will, the man is fully and perfectly free, according to the primary and common notion of freedom" (p. 164).

Having explained his own conceptions of the will and of liberty, Edwards now stated the doctrines of liberty held by "Arminians, Pelagians, and others who oppose the Calvinists."

"These several things," he said, "belong to their notion of liberty: 1. That it consists in a self-determining power in the will, or a certain sovereignty the will has over itself, and its own acts, whereby it determines its own volitions; so as not to be dependent in its determinations, on any cause without itself, nor determined by anything prior to its own acts; 2. Indifference belongs to liberty in their notion of it, or that the mind, previous to the act of volition be *in equilibrio*; 3. Contingence is another thing that belongs and is essential to it . . . as opposed to all necessity, or any fixed and certain connection with some previous ground of its existence. They suppose the essence of liberty so much to consist in these things, that unless the will of man be free in this sense, he has not real freedom, how much soever he may be free to act according to his will'' (pp. 164-165).

To refute these Arminian ideas about the will with reference to moral responsibility, he included a definition of a moral agent in this section of the book on the will and liberty. "A moral agent is," he said, " a being that is capable of those actions that have a moral quality, and which can properly be denominated good or evil in a moral sense, virtuous or vicious, commendable or faulty. To moral agency belongs a moral faculty, or sense of moral good and evil, or of such a thing as desert or worthiness, of praise or blame, reward or punishment; and a capacity which an agent has of being influenced in his actions by moral inducements or motives, exhibited to the view of understanding and reason, to engage to a conduct agreeable to the moral faculty" (p. 165).

It remained for Edwards to attempt to demolish what he took to be the Arminian concepts of the will and to show that, contrary to the Arminian view, a man's actions are properly subject to reward and punishment, praise and blame, even if the will is not free.

Taking up the first of his list of the Arminian ideas on this point, Edwards proposed to "consider the notion of a self-determining power in the will: wherein, according to the Arminians, does most essentially consist the will's freedom; and shall particularly inquire, whether it be not plainly absurd, and a manifest inconsistence, to suppose that the will itself determines all the free acts of the will" (p. 171). He then proceeded to interpret the Arminian view of self-determination in such a way as to reveal its absurdity and inconsistency.

According to Edwards' own view, as has been seen, an act of volition is determined by the desirability of an object as it appears to the mind at the moment of choosing. In this process of choosing only one act occurs. The Arminian conception of self-determination, on the other hand, as Edwards interprets it, contains an implication of two acts of volition. First, the will decides *which* choice will be made; next, the choice which has been decided upon is made. This act of choosing or volition has been determined by the preceding decision about the choice, which had really also been an act of volition. If this first decision as to the choice is really, then, an act, as is the second, i.e., making the choice, it must likewise have been determined by another decision which has determined it. No matter how far back this series of volitions or acts of the will is run, it is impossible to find a point at which an act can be found which has not been determined. Since, then, all volitions must, on the Arminian supposition as interpreted by Edwards, be determined, it is absurd to speak of a "self-determining power of the will" (pp. 171-174).

Although Edwards admitted that the Arminian idea contained the implication that there are causes of volitions, he considered that the causes were not recognized and explained. According to the Arminian scheme, Edwards thought, "then all comes to this, that nothing at all determines the will; volition having absolutely no cause or foundation, of its existence, either within, or without. There is a great noise made about a self-determining power as the source of all free acts of the will:

151

but when the matter comes to be explained, the meaning is, that no power at all is the source of these acts, neither self-determining power, nor any other, but they rise from nothing; no cause, no power, no influence being at all concerned in the matter'' (p. 179).

The Arminian theory implies, therefore, as Edwards saw it, ''that the particular determination of volition is without any cause; because they hold the free acts of the will to be *contingent* events; and contingence is essential to freedom in their notion of it'' (p. 179). Since Edwards believed that the Arminian doctrine of contingence meant that volitions could occur without causes, and he himself thought that volitions are events and that for all events, natural and moral, there are causes, he devoted a chapter to the proposition: ''No Event without a Cause.''

Edwards' own thinking was profoundly influenced by the principle of causation as operative in both the natural and the moral world. In the present inquiry he used the word ''cause'' ''to signify any antecedent, either natural or moral, positive or negative, on which an event . . . so depends, that it is the ground and reason, either in whole or in part, why it is, rather than not; or why it is as it is, rather than otherwise . . .'' ''Having thus explained what I mean by cause, I assert,'' he said, ''that nothing ever comes to pass without a cause'' (pp. 180-181).

It is on account of our perception of cause and effect that we can have some knowledge of the natural world, which is a world of order and regularity. A world in which events could occur spontaneously, or without cause, would be incomprehensible.

Edwards thought that if it were possible for acts of the will to take place without a cause, then it should be possible for natural events to happen without a cause. **This of course he considered an absurdity, however.**

"So that," he said, "it is as repugnant to reason, to suppose that an act of the will should come into existence without a cause, as to suppose the human soul,... or the globe of the earth, or the whole universe, should come into existence without a cause. And if we once allow, that such a sort of effect as a volition may come to pass without a cause, how do we know that many other sorts of effects may not do so too?" (p. 185).

As we have seen, the basis of the Arminian doctrine of the will was that there is, before a choice is made, a period of indifference during which the mind can ponder the matter before it. The opportunity for consideration is necessary if the will is free and if volitions are to be held worthy of praise or blame. If volitions are determined, they would be produced instantaneously when the object is presented to the mind, and there would therefore be no interval provided for consideration before choosing or refusing, and no freedom.

Samuel Johnson had stated this view of the will emphatically, as follows: "I say, freely; for freedom or liberty consisteth in having a power to act or not to act, as we please, and consequently to suspend judging or acting, till we have taken opportunity to make as deliberate and exact a judgment as ever we can, what is best for us in the whole, to do or forbear; as necessity, on the other hand, considered as opposed to liberty, implieth, that it is out of our power to suspend acting, or do otherwise than we do, in which case there can be neither praise nor blame" (II, 421).

In seeking to refute this theory of the period of indifference before decision, Edwards used two principal approaches. In the first place, if the Arminian view has any validity, the indifference during the period of deliberation "must be *perfect* and *absolute*; there must be a perfect freedom from all antecedent preponderation and inclination." "The least degree of antecedent bias must be inconsistent with their notion of liberty" (pp. 204-205). Since there always is an antecedent preponderation and inclination which cannot be eliminated, there is no such thing as perfect indifference.

Besides showing that perfect indifference is impossible, Edwards now tried to demonstrate that postponement of choice in order to exercise deliberation before making a decision would also involve an act of the will: "That this *suspending* of volition, if there properly be any such thing, is itself an act of volition. If the mind determines to suspend its act, it determines it voluntarily; it chooses, on some consideration, to suspend it." This act of suspension was, of course, the matter on which the whole controversy really rested since it was supposed to provide the interval during which a free choice is made. Edwards contended that it could not be shown that there is any moment of complete freedom without any volition before a choice regarding an object is made, since at each instant the indecision itself is an action of the will (p. 210). Such a doctrine as this was, of course, completely inacceptable to the Arminians, since under it, men could not be held responsible for their acts and could not be subject to praise or blame, reward or punishment.

Edwards, however, emphatically dismissed causation from consideration. "The essence of the virtue and vice of dispositions of the heart, and acts of the will," he said, "lies not in their cause, but their nature."

The basis of the opposing view was, he thought, "a supposition, that the virtuousness of the dispositions or acts of the will consists not in the nature of these dispositions or acts, but wholly in the origin or cause of them: so that if the disposition of the mind or act of the will be never so good, yet if the cause of the disposition or act be not our virtue, there is nothing virtuous or praiseworthy in it; and on the contrary, if the

154

will in its inclination or acts be never so bad, yet unless it arises from something that is our vice or fault, there is nothing vicious or blameworthy in it" (p. 337). "Now, if this matter be well considered, it will appear to be altogether a mistake, yea, a gross absurdity; and that it is most certain, that if there be any such things, as a virtuous, or vicious disposition, or volition of the mind, the virtuousness or viciousness of them consists not in the origin or cause of them, but in the nature of them" (p. 337).

The source of evil actions is an evil heart. "When a thing is *from* a man, in that sense, that it is from his will or choice, he is to blame for it, because his will is *in it*; so far as the will is *in it*, blame is *in it*, and no further." In determining blameworthiness, "there is no consideration of the original of that bad will" (p. 427).

Because of the fact that volitions are determined, men act under moral necessity. Although they may be excused for failures due to natural necessity, which lies in factors separate from the will, such as physical obstacles, they cannot be excused because of moral necessity. Natural necessity may force men to do something *against* their will, which is therefore excusable. Moral necessity, however, lies in "the propensity of the will," and acts due to a propensity to evil are therefore not excusable (p. 360).

To account for this propensity of the will toward evil, Edwards gave an explanation which was theological rather than philosophical. His explanation, of course, lies in the Calvinistic doctrine of total depravity. According to this doctrine the will is, on account of the fall of man, so vitiated that it cannot, in its natural state, make right choices. Depravity is due to the fact that God withdrew the influence of the Holy Spirit from all except the elect after the fall of men. Since the fall only those who are provided with the assistance of the Holy

Spirit, i.e., the regenerate, are capable of an inclination toward the good. According to the Arminian view, men are not responsible if they are incapable of good volitions on account of depravity. The sinfulness is God's fault, not man's. Also, the Arminians thought that if all events, including moral, are caused, and all causation can be traced back to God, so God is the author of sin. Edwards' answer to this was that God is not the *author* of sin by positive action, but that by withdrawing the influence of the spirit he permitted sin to come into being. He permitted sin, however, only because good might come of it. Of this the greatest instance is the crucifixion of Christ, which was a horrible sin, but incalculable good came of it.

Although Edwards' treatment of moral responsibility was largely theological, he had prepared the way for it by a mainly philosophical treatment of the will and of causation. There had been complaint, he said, that the Calvinistic writers were too metaphysical, and he therefore felt it necessary to defend metaphysics. "And indeed," he asserted, "we can have no strict demonstration of anything, excepting mathematical truths, but by metaphysics. We can have no proof, that is properly demonstrative, of any one proposition, relating to the being and nature of God, his creation of the world, the dependence of things on Him, the nature of bodies or spirits, the nature of our own souls, or any of the great truths of morality and natural religion, but what is metaphysical." "I am willing," he said, "my arguments should be brought to the test of the strictest and justest reason, and that a clear, distinct and determinate meaning of the terms I use, should be insisted on; but let not the whole be rejected, as if all were confuted, by fixing on it the epithet 'metaphysical'" (p. 424).

Edwards considered that in his metaphysical study

of the will he had provided support for all the five points of Calvinism.

The moral government of the world, he thought, requires that there be "a determining disposal of all events, of every kind, throughout the universe . . . Indeed such an *universal, determining providence* infers some kind of necessity of all events; such a necessity as implies an infallible previous fixedness of the futurity of the event" (p. 431).

On this basis Edwards took up the various points, beginning with the doctrine of depravity. Since everything, natural or moral, happens by necessity, "this doctrine," Edwards said, "supposes *no other necessity* of sinning, than a moral necessity . . . and supposes *no other inability* to obey . . . but a moral inability."

In similar terms Edwards explained the doctrine of irresistible grace. "By irresistible," he said, "is meant, that which is attended with moral necessity." In further explanation he added "that God gives virtue, holiness and conversion to sinners, by an influence which determines the effect, in such a manner, that the effect will infallibly follow by a moral necessity; which is what Calvinists mean by efficacious and irresistible grace" (p. 434).

Edwards next considered the doctrine of "God's *universal* and *absolute* decree . . . and the doctrine of *absolute, eternal personal election* in particular." "God," he said, "orders all events . . . by such a decisive disposal, that the events are infallibly connected with His disposal." Furthermore, God "orders and decides things *knowingly* and *on design*," and never "accidentally and unawares." "And if there be a foregoing *design* of doing and ordering as He does, this is the same with purpose or *decree*." Since the universal decree is God's design for all events, the election of individuals for salvation or damnation, is merely one part of that design. God

makes true saints "by an efficacious power and influence of his, that decides and fixes the event." If God
makes some saints and not others, this, like everything
else that happens, is done by his "eternal design or
decree" (pp. 434-435).

Closely related to the doctrine of election is that of
limited atonement, and so Edwards considered it in his
explanation. "As appears by what has . . . been shewn,"
he said, "God has the actual salvation or redemption
of a certain number in his proper and absolute design,
and of a certain number only. . . . God pursues a proper
design of the salvation of the elect in giving Christ to
die, and pursues such a design with respect to no other"
(p. 435).

The last of the Calvinistic points to be explained in
terms of Edwards' philosophy is the doctrine of the perseverance of the saints. This doctrine he treated in relation to the irresistible grace and election. If conversion,
or becoming a saint, is effected by "the determining
efficacious grace of God, it may well be argued, that it
is so also with respect to men's being continued saints,
or persevering in faith and holiness." Also if the elect
have been destined to a life of holiness and to eternal
salvation, "their appointment to salvation must . . . be
absolute, and not depending on their contingent self-
determining will. Hence it is absolutely fixed in God's
decree, that all true saints shall persevere to actual
eternal salvation" (pp. 436-437).

Edwards considered that the doctrines which he had
explained and defended were those of the Reformation.
Its leaders were, he thought, treated with a certain
amount of supercilious contempt in the present age
which considered itself more enlightened than previous
periods. Many of these modern men who thought that
the leaders of the Reformation had been limited in their

outlook were themselves, Edwards thought, shallow and irresponsible.

In defending the doctrines of the Reformation, however, Edwards himself utilized material that was provided by his own age and that had not been available to earlier generations of Calvinists. He leaned heavily on John Locke for his psychology, although he did not accept all of Locke's ideas uncritically or without modification. Also Edwards' sense of the laws of nature owed much to the improved state of natural science in the eighteenth century. Exact formulation of laws of nature such as those made by Newton are a necessary part of the background for Edwards' use of the principle of the causation of events in both the natural and moral worlds.

The advance which Edwards had made over his predecessors was later noted by Jonathan Edwards, Jr., who thought that his father had provided Calvinists with a new weapon for the defense of their doctrines. "On the great subject of *Liberty* and *Necessity*," he said, "Mr. Edwards made very important improvements. Before him, the Calvinists were nearly driven out of the field, by *Arminians, Pelagians,* and *Socinians.* . . . The Calvinists themselves began to be ashamed of their own cause and to give it up, so far at least as relates to liberty and necessity. . . . But Mr. Edwards put an end to this seeming triumph of those who were thus hostile to that system of doctrines. . . . Now, therefore, the Calvinists find themselves placed upon firm and high ground. They fear not the attacks of their opponents. They face them on the ground of reason, as well as of Scripture."

The younger Edwards wrote as if his father had been victorious in his attack on Arminianism. Such was, however, far from the case. The liberal theological movement continued without cessation and the liberal divines either assumed or stated without much argument the doctrine of free-will.

Although Edwards' *Freedom of the Will* did not stop the development of liberal theology, it was not answered until sixteen years after it was published. In 1770 James Dana, minister at Wallingford, Connecticut, published *An Examination of the Late Reverend President Edwards' "Enquiry on Freedom of Will": More Especially the Tendency and Consequences of the Reasoning therein Contained.* In 1773 Dana followed this with *The Examination of the Late Rev'd President Edwards' Enquiry on Freedom of Will, continued.*

Dana objected to both Edwards' philosophical method and his doctrines.

Explaining why "no animadversions" on Edwards' book had yet been published, he said that "it was to be presumed, that few who might read it would bestow enough attention to understand it; and of those who should attentively read and understand it, few would admit its foundation principles." He admitted that he himself "was discouraged with *only reading* this elaborate and intricate performance some years since." "Yet," he said, "from the great reputation of Mr. *Edwards,* and the prevalence of his doctrine, he came to a resolution of giving the book another and attentive reading." In consequence of this reading, "the following remarks were drawn up." Then, using some of Edwards' characteristic terms, he said: "The 'motive' of his [Dana's] writing is a perswasion of the falsehood of Mr. Edwards' 'scheme,' and this perswasion he 'grants and sees is *necessary,*' he 'cannot help this judgment.'" "And," Dana continued, "as he hath no manner of doubt but the foundation principles of the book . . . are false, so he esteems them of most dangerous tendency." "In a *speculative* and *metaphysical* view, the subject hath been largely discussed by some of the ablest writers," but that "for such reasoning" he himself had "neither abilities, inclination or leisure" and that therefore "his principal aim" was "to consider the subject in a practical view." "The principal purpose metaphysics can serve on practical subjects is," he asserted, "to obscure them" (pp. III-IV).

Thus, as Edwards had anticipated, one of the objections raised against his book concerned his use of metaphysics.

Commenting further on this topic, Dana said, "We do not deny but Mr. Edwards was worthy of the name of a *Philosopher*." "But," he added, "we appeal to the publick, whether some of the most famed *Philosophers* in the English nation, for many years back, and at this day, have not philosophized themselves into scepticism?" Then, with reference to Hume, Dana had this to say: "One of the first distinction in particular (whose essays on some moral subjects are so nearly akin to Mr. *Edwards's* on necessity, that a reader might think the latter copied from the former) appears plainly to be a disbeliever in natural religion, not less than revealed" (p. 126). Again deploring the similarity between Edwards' doctrine and that of the European skeptics, Dana said, "It is a matter of notoriety, that some writers in Europe, who have of late years distinguished themselves in the cause of irreligion and scepticism . . . have built on the same foundation of necessity. 'Tis to be lamented, when the friends and public teachers of religion adopt and set themselves to defend, a scheme of doctrine which gives countenance to infidelity" (*Examination, . . . continued*, p. 71).

Dana objected, also, to Edwards' method of reasoning: "To treat of moral causes and effects in the same manner as a philosopher wou'd discourse on natural causes, is a method of handling moral subjects altogether improper but much used by Mr. Edwards" (*Examination . . . continued*, p. 75).

To illustrate the futility of Edwards' reasoning, Dana

quoted the following passage from the portion of Milton's *Paradise Lost* in which the various activities of the fallen angels are described:

Others apart sat on a hill retired,
In thoughts more elevate, and reason'd high
Of Providence, foreknowledge, will and fate,
Fix'd fate, free will, foreknowledge absolute,
And found no end, in wand'ring mazes lost.
(*Examination . . . continued,* p. 96).

With reference to the doctrinal content of Edwards' book, Dana had one basic objection. In the *Examination . . . continued,* he said, "The examiner begs the reader to keep in mind this single question, *Whether Mr. Edwards's doctrine makes God the efficient cause of all moral wickedness?* He is himself clear in the affirmative of this question." This was the main reason, he said, why he had "undertaken to examine Mr. Edwards's book" (p. vi). "If . . . it should appear that Mr. Edwards's scheme of necessity may justly be charged with making an holy and good God the proper cause of sin, (which is the leading objection we have all along had to his book on the will) it can be of very little purpose to alledge texts of scripture in support of it. A doctrine so repugnant to our natural apprehension of God and His providence cannot be supported by any pretense of authority from him" (p. 106).

Dana also thought that Edwards' view of the origin of sin was at variance with traditional Calvinism: "It is with no great propriety, that Mr. Edwards makes it the caption of almost every section, that his foundation principles are the doctrines of Calvinism; and the opposite of *Arminianism, Pelagianism,* &c." "But in truth," he asked, "when have Calvinists maintain'd, that the vicious wills of moral agents are derived from God, and unalterably fixed by his efficiency? that the first existence of sin arose from the withholding his influence and

162

assistance?'' "Should it also appear that Mr. Edwards's doctrine leaves no room for a distinction between rational and animal creatures in respect of liberty and agency—that it concludes in favour of the mechanism of the human mind, this is a basis on which Calvinists have not built their scheme of doctrine" (*Examination . . . continued,* p. vi).

In summarizing his critical treatment of Edwards' doctrines, Dana said: "Three things have been proposed in the examination of this system: First an inquiry into the supposed volition with the highest motive. Secondly, The indissoluble connection of moral causes and effects. And thirdly, an attempt to shew, that internal moral liberty, as distinguished from external or animal, belongs to moral agents . . . [and] that Mr. Edwards's scheme of necessity, if admitted in theory, is not applicable to practice." (*Examination . . . continued,* p. 137).

In criticism of Edwards' idea that volitions are determined by the highest motive Dana said "that if the highest motive were allowed to be the *next* and *immediate* cause of volition, this is no resolution of the question, as it doth not shew the *original* and *true* cause thereof. The enquiry is not pursued to the end, the *foundation* of the will's determination is not discovered. What it is that gives causal influence to motive, or wherein its energy consists, remains still to be pointed out" (*Examination . . . continued,* pp. 137-138).

In reply to Edwards' conception of the "indissoluble connection of moral causes and effects," Dana answered "that the running up moral events, like natural through a chain of second causes to the first, is confounding the agency of intelligent creatures with mechanism." This doctrine makes the "volitions and conduct of men the agency of Deity, . . . or rather," Dana thought, "upon the principles of Mr. Edwards, the Deity himself is not

163

an agent, but an instrument of necessity and fate."
Hence, according to this scheme, "There is no self-mover
. . . direction . . . determination, or source of activity,
in the universe" (p. 138).

Dana then gave a summary statement of his own positive point of view, which was, he thought, "more consonant to reason and truth" than Edwards'. He considered that he had shown that "from the discernment that
distinguisheth moral agents from the brute-creation, and
their capacity of chusing and acting otherwise than they
in fact do, that internal moral liberty and self-determination belong to them." Edwards had said that volitions
are determined by motives. Dana, on the other hand,
declared "that it no way interferes with this liberty to
admit the exhibition and influence of motives in moral
volitions" (p. 138).

"The scheme of necessity exhibited in Mr. Edwards's
book, if true in speculation, was, upon the whole, shown
false in its practical application—of most dangerous
tendency and consequence." Dana's chief practical objections to Edwards' doctrines were that they made God
the author of sin and that they tended to lead to scepticism. He also thought that he had shown that Edwards
agreed "in his leading sentiments, with antient and modern fatalists" (p. 139).

The point of view which Dana rejected was defended
in Stephen West's *Essay on Moral Agency*, published in
1772. West's argument is almost identical with Edwards'.

He too believed that volitions are caused by motives;
that each volition is an event in a continuous chain or
series, "each successive volition growing, as it were,
out of its next preceeding one as its cause;" that "virtue
and vice . . . consist with the nature of internal dispositions and inclinations of men, in distinction from their
cause."

In refuting the doctrine of self-determination of the

will, West made a distinction between two kinds of power or capacity: the capacity or power to receive influence or be acted upon and a power to exert influence. West thought that to mere common sense the tendency of natural bodies to gravitate toward the center might be due to "some influence exerted *by the bodies themselves, upon themselves*" rather than to some power acting upon them. As it is with inanimate bodies, so it is with volitions. "For a person to be a subject *capable of having exercises of the will,* and for him to *originate* these exercises, are two very different things. . . . The one is a power to *operate;* the other a power *to be wrought upon*: the one, puts forth power and exerciseth influence in order to produce effects; the other, is a fitness or adaptedness to have effects of a certain kind appear in it" (p. 43). Men have the capacity to have exercises of the will produced in them, but not the power to produce these exercises.

One of Dana's strongest objections to Edwards' system, as has been noted, was that it really implied "that God is the *efficient* cause of sin" (*Examination . . . continued,* p. 73).

West did not find such an implication objectionable. He "enquired into, and particularly considered" the question of "the divine agency and disposal respecting the taking place of sin in the system" and "whether the existence and taking place of *moral evil* are not the occasion of *more and greater good,* in the system, than could otherwise have been effected and produced" (pp. 169, 173). His conclusion was that "it was, upon the whole, a *desirable* thing, that *moral evil* should come into existence" (p. 202) and "that such a *positive divine agency and disposal* as would give infallible certainty that moral evil should come into existence in the system; are not inconsistent with the purity and holiness of God" (p. 214).

By this time, as will be seen, a view of sin such as West expressed had become one of the characteristic doctrines of some of Edwards' followers, whose theology, known as the New Divinity, was largely derived from the *Treatise Concerning Religious Affections* and *The Freedom of the Will.*

VI

JONATHAN EDWARDS, THE NEW DIVINITY, AND THE "MORAL SENSE"

Although Edwards considered that his chief task in combatting Arminianism was to refute the doctrine of freedom of the will, another matter soon occupied his attention. It was his belief that virtue lies in the disposition of the will, that only those who have been converted by the influence of the Spirit can have a proper disposition of the will, and that the only true virtue is true holiness. Because of this he found it necessary to attack a type of moral philosophy best represented by Francis Hutcheson according to which all men are endowed with a "moral sense" which enables them to perceive virtue and that all men are capable, at least to some degree, of virtuous action. In 1755, the year after the publication of *The Freedom of the Will,* Edwards criticized this view and presented his own moral philosophy in a short treatise entitled *The Nature of True Virtue.* This was not published, however, until 1765, and will be discussed later in connection with a theological movement which had developed in the meantime.

This theological movement—called the New Divinity, and later Hopkinsianism—was an outgrowth of some of Edwards' ideas, especially some of the points which had been stated in *A Treatise Concerning Religious A,,* *tions.*

The points in Edwards' work which are basic to the New Divinity are the first four of the signs of "gracious affections":

1. "Affections that are truly spiritual and gracious do arise from those influences on the heart which are spiritual, supernatural and divine."

2. "The first objective ground of gracious affections is the transcendently excellent and amiable nature of divine things, as they are in themselves; and not any conceived relation they bear to self or self interest."

3. "Those affections that are truly holy, are primarily founded on the loveliness of the moral excellency of divine things. Or . . . a love to divine things for the beauty and sweetness of their moral excellency is the first beginning of all holy affections."

4. "Gracious affections do arise from the mind's being enlightened, richly and spiritually to apprehend divine things." In the explanation of this point Edwards said that, just as there is an esthetic taste, "so there is likewise such a thing as a divine taste . . . in the hearts of the saints, whereby they are . . . led and guided in discerning the true spiritual beauty of actions . . ."

The first of the writers to follow the line pointed out by Edwards was Joseph Bellamy, of Bethlehem, Connecticut, who had studied divinity with Edwards at Northampton. Bellamy had, like Edwards, been disappointed with the results of the revival, and had therefore undertaken, with the help of Edwards' writings, to discover and explain the essence of religion. The first result of this effort was *The Nature of True Religion Delineated,* published in 1750.

Stating his basic thesis, Bellamy said: "True religion consists in a conformity to the *law* of God, and in a compliance with the *gospel* of Christ." Following Edwards

167

rather closely, Bellamy insisted that a correct speculative view of God and the law is insufficient, but that one must have "a spiritual sight of God, and a sense of his glory and beauty," which "begets love." One must have a *"temper of mind* or *frame of heart* perfectly answerable to the *moral law*; the *moral law* being, as it were, *a transcript of the moral perfections of God."* The natural man Bellamy thought to be incapable of such understanding and acceptance of the moral law. The right view and temper could be produced only by a *"divine light,* imparted by the spirit of God to the soul . . ."* "This *spiritual* and *divine light* . . . shines in the heart, and consists in the *knowledge* of *Glory,* . . . that is, in a *sense* of *moral beauty*; a *sense* of that beauty there is in the *moral* perfections of *God,* and in all spiritual and divine things . . ."

Before Bellamy published his next work, Edwards' *Freedom of the Will* had appeared. The idea set forth in this book, that God had, for a good purpose, permitted sin to come into the world, was made the subject of Bellamy's next work, entitled *The Wisdom of God in the Permission of Sin,* published in 1758. He had argued in his previous book that true religion means acceptance of the moral law with both mind and heart. Embracing the moral law, he now said, involves approval of God's whole moral government.

A deterrent to such approval is the existence of sin, which some men, on account of their limited views, are prone to think might have been prevented. To correct this misunderstanding, he presented the following doctrine: "A sight of the wisdom of God in the permission of sin, is very useful to promote holiness of heart and life." To show how God can permit evil and then make glorious use of it, he related the story of Joseph and its eventual relation to the scheme of redemption. In this story, he said, "we have HUMAN NATURE brought upon the stage and experiments made upon the heart of man, in a great variety; whereby its true temper is as certainly determined as was ever anything in the natural world, by the great *Sir Isaac Newton.*"

In further explanation, Bellamy made use of the concept of universal order and also of the concept of the "sense of moral beauty" and of the "sense of the moral perfections of God" which he had derived from Edwards and which he had presented in his first book. "As all God's works are uniform, so," he said, "we may justly argue, from the wisdom and beauty of particular parts, to the wisdom and beauty of the whole." Although the rightness of a system which includes sin may not be readily apparent to us, "yet we have seen by strict demonstration, that, of all possible plans, this is the best." God, who had complete freedom of choice, absolute power, and perfect wisdom, was free to create or not to create. He chose to create. "And of all systems, he had his choice. . . . Nor was it possible he should make a mistake; all things were open and naked before him; he knew which was best; and he chose this . . ." If we do not see the rightness of the plan, it is because of "our not seeing the whole plan, or our want of good taste, or both . . ." "Besides the narrowness of our present views, our taste, too, is at present much vitiated. The best of men in the world are far from that high relish for moral beauty which is needful to render them good judges, on a plan so altogether holy and divine as this must certainly be."

Bellamy concluded that the outcome of the permission of sin was "to bring more honour to God, and to make the good part of creation more humble, holy, and happy." To illustrate this he considered the case of the angels. When the good angels saw Satan and his hosts, once their fellow-citizens bound in chains of despair and waiting for the day of judgment when they were to be

169

doomed to the most intolerable pains of hell, they would realize the horrible wickedness and dreadful nature of rising in rebellion against God. The humility, holiness, and happiness of the good angels was thus increased, he estimated, "a hundred, a thousand, perhaps ten thousand fold."

The next year, 1759, Samuel Hopkins, another former pupil of Edwards, presented a similar view in a book entitled *Sin, Through Divine Intervention, an Advantage to the Universe, and Yet no Excuse or Encouragement to It.*

This view of sin as advantageous and as providing an opportunity for God to manifest his glory became a standard doctrine in the New Divinity which was in process of formation. It was, however, found obnoxious by traditional Calvinists and was soon attacked.

Bellamy's book was answered in 1759 by Samuel Moody, a firm Calvinist, in *An Attempt to Point Out the Evil and Pernicious Consequences of Rev. Joseph Bellamy's Recent Doctrines Respecting Moral Evil.* Moody denied that it was one of God's main purposes to plan for his own glory or that sin had been advantageous to the whole system. His main objection to sin was that it produced disorder, especially social disorder. In discussing this point Moody made use of the terminology and concepts of esthetics much as Edwards had done in a different context. "Had all rational Beings continued holy and perfect," he said, "there would have been now compleat Order and Harmony thro' the Universe. . . . We know that Order and Symmetry are the Beauty of things natural and artificial. . . . In well constituted Societies, civil and religious, where all members keep their Places and discharge the Duties appointed them; the Result is Harmony, Strength, and Happiness. But as soon as they leave their Spheres and violate the Laws of the Community, Confusion and Misery follow."

Bellamy replied the next year, 1760, with *The Wisdom of God in the Permission of Sin Vindicated* in which he gave particular attention to the doctrine that this is the best of all possible worlds.

In 1762 he summarized his general views in *An Essay upon the Nature and Glory of the Gospel.* In this he asserted, as he had implied in his first book: "That the divine law is holy, just, good, and glorious, antecedent to a consideration of the gift of Christ," and "That it is seen to be such by every enlightened soul."

Since only an "enlightened soul" can perceive the divine law properly, Bellamy wrote a chapter on "The Nature of Divine Illumination." In this he made use of a parallel between the esthetic sense and the spiritual sense as Edwards had done in his *Treatise Concerning Religious Affections.* On the sense of beauty, however, he cited not Edwards, but Hutcheson. "That the idea of a natural beauty supposes an internal sense, implanted by our Creator, by which the mind is capacitated to discern such kind of beauty, is," he said, "clearly illustrated and proved by a late ingenious philosopher." Although Bellamy found Hutcheson's concept of the sense of beauty satisfactory, he turned to Edwards as his authority on the spiritual sense. "And," he said, "that the idea of spiritual beauty supposes an internal spiritual sense, communicated to the soul by the spirit of God, in the work of the new creation, is also as clearly illustrated and proved, by a late divine, whose praise is in all the churches" (*Works,* II, 503).

There is significance in the fact that Bellamy turned to Edwards rather than to Hutcheson for a concept of the "spiritual sense." The difference between the "spiritual sense" of Edwards and the "moral sense" of Hutcheson provides one of the reasons why the moral sense philosophy was not acceptable to the New Divinity men. It was, however, utilized by their New England opponents. The moral sense as set forth by Hutcheson is possessed by all men; the spiritual sense, or taste, as presented by Edwards and his followers is possesed only by those who are illuminated by a divine and supernatural light.

In assuming that all men have a moral sense which is reliable Hutcheson and others had ignored the doctrine of total depravity. This doctrine had also been attacked by John Taylor in *The Scripture-Doctrine of Original Sin Proposed to a Free and Candid Examination,* published in 1738. Taylor's book was answered by Edwards in *The Great Christian Doctrine of Original Sin Defended* (1758).

Meanwhile Edwards had prepared two more treatises entitled *The Nature of True Virtue* and *Concerning the End for which God Created the World,* which were published posthumously as *Two Dissertations* under the editorial supervision of Samuel Hopkins.

Although Edwards' defense of the doctrine of original sin was primarily a refutation of the theological treatise of Taylor, he also saw that the moral sense philosophy contained an implied threat to the doctrine. His *Nature of True Virtue,* although primarily an ethical treatise intended to offset the effects of the moral sense school, was indirectly a defense of the doctrine of depravity and is therefore related to his book on original sin.

Edwards himself made the connection clear in a statement in *The Great Christian Doctrine of Original Sin Defended.*

After answering various theological objections to the doctrine of depravity, Edwards said: "As to the arguments, made use of by many late writers, from the universal *moral sense,* and the reasons they offer from experience, and observation of the *nature* of mankind, to show that we are *born* into the world with principles of *virtue*; with a natural prevailing relish, approbation,

172

and love of righteousness, truth, and goodness, and of whatever tends to the public welfare; with a prevailing natural disposition to dislike, to resent and condemn what is selfish, unjust and immoral; and a native bent in mankind to mutual benevolence, tender compassion, &c., those who have had such objections against the doctrine of Original Sin thrown in their way, and desire to see them particularly considered, I ask leave to refer them to a *Treatise on the Nature of True Virtue*, lying by me prepared for the press, which may erelong be exhibited to public view" (II, 508).

Before Edwards' *Nature of True Virtue* was published, Samuel Hopkins, in a letter to Thomas Foxcroft dated January 9, 1761, took notice of the above passage and of the relation of Edwards' treatise to the doctrine of original sin. "I believe," he said, "Mr. Edwards supposed that his treatise on 'The Nature of True Virtue' fully answered what he promises in his book on Original Sin. He supposed that by showing what true virtue *is*, and as a consequence of this, what is *not* virtue, he effectually answers all the objections there mentioned, and put a sufficient and full answer into the mouth of every one who should have such objections thrown in his way, though he does not mention the objections in that treatise, or answer them as being made against the doctrine of Original Sin." Although Edwards "particularly considers, and proves, which he does in that treatise . . . that *Arminians'* virtue, such as their *moral* sense, &c., is no virtue at all," all the objections to the doctrine of original sin are really answered by this one point.

The moral philosophy which Edwards and his followers found in some way similar to their own but in other more important ways totally unacceptable is best represented in Francis Hutcheson's *The Original of Our Ideas of Beauty and Virtue* (published in 1725, second ed. 1738).

Influenced by ideas presented in Lord Shaftesbury's *Characteristics* (1711), Hutcheson based his ethical system on the theory that men have internal senses as well as senses for perceiving physical phenomena. The "power of perceiving the Beauty of Regularity, Order, Harmony" is an *"Internal Sense"*—the sense of Beauty and "that Determination to *approve* Affections, Actions, or Characters of rational Agents, which we call virtuous" is a "MORAL SENSE" (pp. xiii, ed. of 1738). "The AUTHOR of Nature," Hutcheson said, "has much better furnish'd us for a virtuous conduct than some *moralists* seem to imagine. . . . He has given us strong AFFECTIONS to be the springs of each virtuous Action; and made Virtue a lovely Form, that we might easily distinguish it from its contrary and be made happy by the Pursuit of it" (p. xiv, ed. of 1738).

"The Word MORAL GOODNESS in this Treatise," Hutcheson said, "denotes our Idea of *some Quality apprehended in Actions, which procures Approbation, attended with Desire of the Agents' Happiness. Moral Evil* denotes our Idea of a *contrary Quality, which excites Condemnation or Dislike"* (p. 105). Taking note of an esthetic quality in moral virtue, Hutcheson said that "we have a distinct Perception of *Beauty* or *Excellence* in the kind Affections of *rational Agents*; whence we are determin'd to admire and love such *Characters* and Persons" (p. 112). Further discussing our response to moral actions, Hutcheson said: "We must . . . certainly have other Perceptions of *moral Actions,* than those of Advantage [i.e., to us]; and that Power of receiving these perceptions may be call'd a *Moral Sense* . . ." (p. 113).

Regarding the source of moral actions, Hutcheson said, "Every Action, which we apprehend as either *morally good* or *evil,* is always suppos'd to flow from some *Affection* toward sensitive Natures" (p. 132). The affections which are of most importance in morals are love and hate. Of love there are two kinds: esteem and love of benevolence. Of hatred there are also two kinds: contempt and hatred of malice (pp. 134-135).

Of the nature of actions which are admired, Hutcheson said: "If we examine all the Actions which are counted *amiable* anywhere, and inquire into the Grounds upon which they are approv'd, we shall find that in the Opinion of the Person who approves them, they always appear as BENEVOLENT, or flowing from *Goodwill* to others" (p. 166).

"BENEVOLENCE is a Word fit enough in general, to denote the internal Spring of Virtue," Hutcheson said. "But to understand this more distinctly, 'tis highly necessary to observe, that under this Name are included very different Dispositions of the Soul. Sometimes it denotes a *calm, extensive Affection,* or Good-will toward all Beings capable of Happiness or Misery: Sometimes, 2. A calm deliberate Affection of the Soul toward the Happiness of certain smaller systems or Individuals; such as Patriotism, or Love of a Country, Friendship, Parental-Affection . . . Or, 3. The several kinds of particular Passions of Love, Pity, Sympathy, Congratulation" (p. 177).

He observed also that "Self-love" is "not excluded by Benevolence." The reason for this is "that every *moral Agent* justly considers himself as a *Part* of this *rational System,* which may be useful to the *Whole*; so that he may be in part an Object of his own universal *Benevolence.* Nay further . . . he may see, that the preservation of the *System* requires every one to be innocently solicitous about himself" (pp. 178-179). Although Hutcheson thought that benevolence could be either universal or extended to "smaller systems or Individuals," he also said that "the Moral Beauty of Actions, or Dispositions, increases according to the Number of Persons

175

to whom the good Effects of them extend" and that "the more limited *Instincts* tend to produce a smaller Moment of Good, because confined to small Numbers" (pp. 185-186).

Even if one has a sentiment of universal benevolence, it cannot be applied equally to all men. This Hutcheson explained by an analogy with a physical law. "The *universal Benevolence* toward all Men, we may compare to that Principle of *Gravitation,* which perhaps extends to all Bodys in the *Universe*; but increases as the Distance is diminish'd, and is strongest when Bodys come to touch each other. Now this *Increase,* upon nearer Approach, is as necessary as that there should be any *Attraction* at all. For a *general Attraction,* equal in all Distances, would by the Contrariety of such Multitudes of equal Forces, put an End to all Regularity of Motion, and perhaps stop it altogether" (pp. 221-222).

Such was the moral philosophy which Edwards felt called upon to refute in the course of his attack on Arminianism. He himself, however, had long held views similar to those of Hutcheson. As a boy at Yale he had thought that harmony and symmetry are the chief characteristics of excellence and that the highest form of harmony is "Being's consent to entity." Love among minds was, he thought, similar to attraction among physical bodies. Later he had made use of the parallel between esthetic taste and spiritual taste. And he had long believed that benevolence is the highest of all virtues. Hutcheson, however, differed from Edwards in that he believed that benevolence extended to lesser groups within the universal system is real virtue although not the highest. In assuming that all men have a moral sense which is reliable, he ignored completely the doctrine of total depravity. Furthermore, he ignored the idea that regeneration is essential for truly virtuous conduct.

In setting forth his ideas of the nature of true virtue

Edwards began with the use of an esthetic concept, explaining that by virtue we mean "something *beautiful,* or rather some kind of *beauty,* or excellency." Not all beauty is called virtue, however—for instance, not the beauty of nature or art—"but some beauty belonging to Beings that have *perception* and *will.*" This beauty is not physical, "but it is a beauty that has its original seat in the mind." "But . . . not *every* thing that may be called a beauty of mind, is properly called virtue." There is, for instance, a "beauty of understanding and speculation," and "there is something in the ideas and conceptions of great philosophers and statesmen, that may be called beautiful." This kind of beauty is, however, not virtue. "But virtue is the beauty of those qualities and acts of the mind, that are of a moral nature . . ." "Things of this sort . . . are not anything belonging merely to speculation; but to the *disposition* and *will,* or . . . the *heart.*"[1]

There are, however, some things which appear to be virtuous which are really not so. This happens because of an imperfect view of them. Things may be considered "partially and superficially" rather than "in their whole nature and the extent of their connections in the universality of things." In explaining this, Edwards said: "There is a general and a particular beauty. By a *particular* beauty, I mean that by which a thing appears beautiful when considered only with regard to its connection with, and tendency to some particular things within a limited, and as it were, a private sphere. And a *general* beauty is that by which a thing appears beautiful when viewed most perfectly, comprehensively and universally, with regard to all its tendencies, and in connection with every thing it stands related to." In view of this distinction, Edwards said: "*That only,* therefore, is what I mean by true virtue, which is that belonging

---

[1] *Works* (New York, 1844), II, 261. Subsequent references are to this edition.

to the *heart* of an intelligent Being, that is beautiful by a *general* beauty, or beautiful in a comprehensive view as it is in itself, and as related to everything that it stands in connection with."

On this basis Edwards formulated the fundamental thesis of his book. "And therefore, when we are inquiring concerning the nature of true virtue, viz., wherein this true and general beauty of the heart does most essentially consist—this is my answer to the inquiry:

"True virtue most essentially consists in benevolence to Being in general. Or perhaps to speak more accurately, it is that consent, propensity and union of heart to Being in general, that is immediately exercised in a general good will" (II, 262).

Edwards understood that in practice not all benevolence was directed to "Being in general" as such, but rather to individuals. This benevolence toward individuals, however, is true virtue *only* if it is related to a sentiment of universal benevolence. It was on this point that Edwards differed radically from the "moral sense" philosophers who thought that benevolence to individuals and smaller groups is real virtue even if it is inferior to universal benevolence.

Edwards' concern with self-interest or benevolence to limited groups or "systems" only could not be true virtue because what might seem good for one's self or for a limited group could very well be quite contrary to what is best for the universal system.

Although he thought that a "true and general beauty of the heart" is required for true virtue, he granted that there is "another inferior secondary beauty" which is "some image" of this primary beauty, and which exists in both spiritual beings and inanimate things. Characterized by symmetry, proportion and harmony, it is seen in regular geometrical figures, and in the "figures on a piece of chints, or brocade" and in "the sweet

178

mutual consent and agreement of the various notes of a melodious tune" (II, 272).

This secondary beauty in material things is not without spiritual significance. In the "consent and agreement" which exist in beautiful things, "there may be some image of the true, spiritual, original beauty." Since "it pleases God to observe analogy in his works . . . he has constituted the external world in an analogy to things in the spiritual world." God established this resemblance between primary and secondary beauty, especially in its highest forms, as in nature and in music, in order "to assist those whose hearts are under the influence of a truly virtuous temper . . . and enliven in them a sense of spiritual beauty" (II, 273). Presumably the unregenerate receive no such assistance from secondary beauty.

This secondary beauty may exist in immaterial as well as in material things. For instance, "there is a beauty of order in society . . . when the different members . . . all have their appointed office, place, and station according to their several capacities, and every one keeps his place, and continues in his proper business." This beauty is analogous to that of a building in which all the pillars and pilasters are set in their proper positions. There is also a beauty in wisdom, which "consists in the united tendency of thoughts, ideas, and particular volitions, to one general purpose," and "in the virtue called justice, which consists in the agreement of different things, that have relation to one another . . . and therefore is the very same sort of beauty with that uniformity and proportion, which is observable in those . . . material things that are esteemed beautiful" (II, 274-275).

This inferior beauty is quite distinct from the superior beauty for which *"union of heart to Being in general"* and "benevolence to being in general" are required. A taste for this secondary beauty is entirely different from a taste for true virtue. In spite of the fact that there is an analogy between secondary beauty and "spiritual and virtuous beauty" to the extent that "material things can have an analogy to things spiritual," men's approbation of inferior beauty is not due to any recognition of this analogy. Hence it "does not spring from any virtuous temper, and has no connection with virtue." In direct opposition to the point of view represented by Hutcheson, Edwards concluded: "A taste of this inferior virtue in things immaterial, is one thing that has been mistaken by some moralists for a true virtuous principle, implanted naturally in the hearts of all mankind" (II, 277).

Edwards granted that there is in men a principle of "natural conscience, which, though it implies no such thing as actual benevolence to Being in general, nor any delight in such a principle . . . and so implies no truly spiritual sense or virtuous taste, yet should approve and condemn the same things that are approved and condemned by a spiritual sense or virtuous taste." Edwards considered that this "natural conscience" was the same as the "moral sense, so much insisted on in the writings of many of late." These writers, he said, had "insisted on a disinterested moral sense, universal in the world of mankind, as an evidence of a disposition to true virtue, consisting in a benevolent temper, naturally implanted in the minds of all men." He granted that these writers had shown that there is such a thing as a moral taste in men, which he took to be merely the natural conscience, or the "sense of moral good and evil." There is nothing in this, however, which "is of the nature of a truly virtuous taste, or determination of mind to relish and delight in the essential beauty of true virtue arising from a virtuous benevolence of heart" (II, 289).

Neither the moral sense nor the spiritual taste is arbitrarily granted to man or is arbitrary in its operations.

Both are grounded on the "reason and nature of things."
For this reason, the "moral sense, if the understanding
be well informed, and be exercised at liberty, and in an
extensive manner, without being restrained to a private
sphere, approves the very same things which a spiritual
and divine taste approves; and those things only: though
not on the same grounds, nor with the same kind of
approbation. Therefore, as that divine sense has been
already shown to be agreeable to the necessary nature
of things, so this inferior moral sense, being so far correspondent to that, must so far agree with the nature
of things" (II, 302-303).

Although this book is written more in philosophical
than Calvinistic theological terms, Edwards' theological
doctrines are of course implicit if not stated in the argument. Since he himself considered that this book was related to his defense of the doctrine of original sin, it
can be assumed that those who are incapable of true
virtue are the unregenerate. It can also be assumed that
those who have a spiritual rather than merely moral
sense are the regenerate to whom a divine and supernatural light has been imparted.

The question as to the possibility of moral virtue in
the acts of the unregenerate at once entered a current
theological dispute between the followers of Edwards
and some moderate Calvinists. This argument concerned
the efficacy of preparatory effort toward conversion by
the unregenerate. Those who denied the value of such
effort based their argument on the doctrine of the depravity of the will. Those who encouraged such efforts
made use of the "moral sense" philosophy.

Joseph Bellamy at once saw that opposing views regarding moral virtue held a central position among the
various points on which the contending parties differed.
In 1766, the year after the publication of Edwards' *True
Virtue,* Bellamy wrote, in a letter of advice to a theo-

logical student: "The occasion of the objections against Edwards's scheme is not understanding him. He wrote especially against the views of Hutchenson [sic.]. They ought to be read first, and Dr. Brown's answer to the *Characteristics* of Lord Shaftesbury (which contains the fundamental sentiments which Mr. Edwards designed to oppose) and enter thoroughly into it. Then read Edwards on the Affections; then Edwards on Virtue, and God's last end, and be at pains to understand the controversy."

In this dispute the chief spokesman for the doctrine that all the efforts of the unregenerate are completely devoid of merit and efficacy was Samuel Hopkins. In 1765, the year in which Edwards' *True Virtue* was published under his supervision, Hopkins published *An Enquiry Concerning the Promises of the Gospel, whether any of them are made to the exercises and doings of those in an unregenerate state.* This was an answer to two sermons on *Striving to Enter in at the Strait Gate,* which had been published in 1761 by Jonathan Mayhew, one of the leading anti-Calvinistic ministers of Boston. Mayhew, with reference to the efforts toward conversion, had said that "there is a certain connexion between sinners striving to obtain the salvation which God has revealed, and their actually obtaining it." "How strange? how unaccountable it is then, that any should assert, as some have done, that there is nothing to be done by sinners, in order to their salvation; or at least nothing besides believing! There are some who assert that all an unregenerate man does or can do, is so far from having any real tendency to promote his salvation, that it is but rebellion against God, and so sets him a still greater distance from Him."

It was on this point of view that Hopkins answered Mayhew. Hopkins described conversion as a "change... wrought by the Spirit of God, immediately and instantaneously . . ." At the time of regeneration, "the light and truth of God's word enters into the mind and it discerns the things of the Spirit of God in their reality, beauty, wisdom, glory; and in this view and sense of divine truth approves of the divine character.''

The efforts of the sinner have had nothing to do, however, with effecting this change. If the awakened sinner who has "taken a great deal of pains in the use of means, and has thereby got a great degree of instruction and knowledge'' still continues to be "impenitent,'' he is "much more guilty and vile, and a greater criminal in God's sight, than if he had never attained to this conviction and knowledge.'' He is "guilty of the abuse of, and opposition to, all this light and knowledge, which he could not be while he had it not.'' "And,'' Hopkins concluded, "awakened, sinners . . . who are most attentive to the use of means, are commonly if not always, really more guilty and odious in God's sight than they who are secure and at ease in their sins.''

It was this view of the uselessness of preparatory effort toward conversion as presented by Hopkins and his school which the liberals found untenable and even abhorrent.

In 1767, Jedediah Mills answered Hopkins in *An Inquiry concerning the State of the Unregenerate under the Gospel*. Speaking of the use of the means of grace, i.e., hearing the Word preached, praying, and reading the Scriptures, Mills said, "It is well known, that these things, as preparatory to a saving faith, in the ordinary way of God's dispensing his grace, have been steadily maintained by Calvinist divines of the greatest note, as agreeable to the oracles of God.''

Since the view represented by Hopkins differed from traditional Calvinism, Mills called it a "new divinity.'' Defining this term, he said: "By the new divinity here, I mean the divinity lately brought into the country . . ., that entirely denies any preparatory work, in order to saving faith, by the common influence of the spirit, affirming, that the first influence of the spirit upon the soul, is of a saving nature; and that it can't be proved from the holy scriptures, that the spirit of God ever strives with the unregenerate." The term "new divinity," first employed as a term of reproach, was for a time used to designate the theology of Hopkins, Bellamy, and others who joined with and followed them. It was later, however, supplanted by the term "Hopkinsianism."

In the same year (1767) of Mills' reply to Hopkins, Moses Hemmenway published *Seven Sermons on the Obligation and Encouragement of the Unregenerate,* which, although not directed at Hopkins, represented a point of view distinctly opposed to his. Hemmenway maintained that the unregenerate were quite able to make good use of the means of grace and to amend and reform their lives. Conversion he described as a gradual process attending such efforts. The basis of the idea that the efforts of the unregenerate are sinful was, he thought, "That the unregenerate act merely from self love in all their religious performances." This, he declared, "is either impious or false." "If," he said, "it only means, that the ultimate end of their acting is the obtainment of something which they regard as good and agreeable to their desire, in this sense we may as truly say, that every creature acts merely from self love. But if the meaning be, that in all that they do they have nothing in view but to advance *their* own private interest and happiness, this is contrary to scripture, reason, and experience." In support of this assertion, Hemmenway made use of the "moral sense" philosophy. "There is," he said, "in human nature a moral taste, or sense of moral good and evil, which does not arise from self love, as the late Mr. *Edwards* has observed, after *Butler, Hutcheson,* and others. See his dissertation on the nature of virtue. This doubtless has its influence on the conduct of men in general, particularly on their religious conduct. . . . The moral sense or conscience, and the social affections are as natural to man as self-preservation. And they are evidently distinct from each other, notwithstanding all that has been urged to the contrary by *Hobbes* or any other. For it is to be observed that the impleaded notion is no other than one of the exploded tenets of *Hobbes*. But it is no service to the cause of truth, for any one to belie human nature, in order to prove that it is depraved; and disown those 'sparks of celestial fire, . . . which remain under the ashes of apostasy' " (pp. 34-35).

In 1768 Hopkins published *Two Discourses*: (1) *On the Knowledge of the Law of God in Order to the Knowledge of Sin,* and (2) *A Particular and Critical Inquiry into the Cause, Nature and Means by which Men are Born of God.* Most of this was a restatement of what Bellamy and Hopkins had said in previous publications. In the second of the sermons, however, Hopkins stated a doctrine, not included in his previous publications, which he derived from Edwards' *Nature of True Virtue.* Using the word "holiness" instead of "virtue," Hopkins said: "As true holiness consists summarily in disinterested kind affection to other beings, God and the creature, or in true love and benevolence to being in general, so sinfulness or corruption of heart summarily consists in the want of benevolence, and that which is directly opposite to this, to wit, selfishness, or as it is sometimes called, *self-love*; by which a person regards and seeks his own private interest, without any true disinterested regard to others." For a more thorough examination of the matter, he referred the reader to Edwards' treatise. From this time on the concept of universal benevolence was to be a leading article in Hopkins' theology.

In the next year, 1769, Hopkins replied to Jedediah
Mills in *The True State and Character of the Unregenerate*, which is primarily a reassertion of his earlier
statement. In addition, however, he accused Mills, who
had professed to state the Calvinistic view, of having
"really taken up Dr. Mayhew's cause." He thought that
Mills' view regarding the efforts of the unregenerate
"contains the substance and soul of the Arminian
scheme, and if followed in all its consequences, will sub-
vert every important doctrine of Calvinism."

Hopkins also objected to Mills' accusation that his
was a *"new* divinity." This had, he said, been "a
grand objection against Christ and his disciples" and
against all attempts at reformation in the church ever
since. To some people, "new, erroneous, and wrong...
are synonymous words." "It is," he said, "no argument
at all that a doctrine is true, because it has long been
received as such; nor is it the least evidence that a doctrine is not agreeable to Scripture, that it is quite new
and has never before been advanced." And therefore
both old and new are to be "examined with equal
caution."

By this time the "new divinity" had acquired the support of two new exponents: Nathaniel Whitaker and
John Smalley. Neither of them contributed any new doctrinal material, but the publications of both of them
were included among those attacked in the next controversial work directed at the new divinity.

This attack was made by William Hart who dealt with
the whole New Divinity group, in a pamphlet entitled
*A Sermon, of a New Kind, Never Preached, nor ever
will be; Containing a Collection of* Doctrines, *Belonging
to the Hopkintonian Scheme of Orthodoxy; Or the Marrow of the Most Modern Divinity. And an Address to
the Unregenerate, Agreeable to the Doctrines* (1769).
The first part is a mock sermon made up of extracts

from recent publications by Bellamy, Hopkins, Smalley, and Whitaker, with a few adverse criticisms in footnotes. One of Hart's chief objections was that "the writers upon the new scheme of orthodoxy, do generally mix, in the composition of their discourses, a large proportion of false metaphysics, by which common readers are bewildered and lost, as in a fog." The second part is also a sermon, intended to show a congregation "what a dark and discouraging aspect this scheme of doctrines has upon you." Hart encouraged his congregation to "desire and pray" for grace, even if the "desire does not spring from the highest motives."

Like Hemmenway, Hart used the moral sense philosophy in support of the doctrine that men are capable of acceptable efforts before conversion. In a dialog entitled *Brief Remarks on a Number of False Propositions and Dangerous Errors Collected from the Discourses of Whitaker and Hopkins*, published in 1769, he said: "There is in man a natural faculty whereby he is rendered capable of discerning and distinguishing between moral good and evil . . . and readily perceives the one to be right, amiable, and worthy of esteem and honor, the other wrong, hateful and blameworthy, immediately, as soon as these objects are seen by the mind in their true light . . . without any further reasoning about them. This faculty is 'innate,' an essential part of the natural constitution of all intelligent and moral beings as such." Hart admitted, however, that while men naturally recognize and love "good actions and agents or characters" as such, they may hate them when they interfere with their own "lust" or "private interest." Likewise the character of God cannot be "hated for its own sake" but only "from interested views."

Hopkins replied to Hart in *Animadversions on Mr. Hart's Late Dialogue*, published in 1770. In this treatise he commended Edwards' *Nature of True Virtue*, "one

design of which," he said, "was to show that men have
no degree of true virtue but are totally corrupt."
"Why," he asked, "did not Mr. H. take this dissertation in hand, and censure and confute it? . . . This
would be doing something to the purpose, to put a stop
to those *dangerous* errors, and laying the ax to the foot
of the tree."

In *A Letter to the Rev. S. Hopkins Occasioned by His
Animadversion,* Hart replied that he had taken Hopkins'
advice to answer Edwards' treatise on true virtue. He
had not yet read the work when he wrote his *Brief
Remarks,* but having done so since, he had found Edwards' "notion of virtue" "new and strange" and the
"scheme" which Hopkins had "built on it" to be "new."
"Both," he said, "must stand or fall together." "I
have," he said, "laid the ax to the foot of the tree as
requested, and perhaps shall publish some remarks upon
it, shewing that Mr. Edwards' notions of virtue, of the
primary and *secondary* beauty of moral actions, &. are
wrong, imaginary, and fatally destructive of the foundations of morality and religion."

Hart's promised reply to Edwards, entitled *Remarks
on President Edwards's Dissertation on True Virtue,*
was published in 1771. In it Hart not only dealt with
Edwards' doctrine but with the whole New Divinity
school in so far as it was derived from Edwards.

He said that the basic doctrine stated in Edwards'
treatise seemed to be "the foundation on which several
doctrines, in the *new* scheme of divinity are built, and
serves as a key to explain them . . . These, in particular, viz. That 'the moral perfections and character of
God, as revealed by the Gospel, and seen by natural men,
under the teachings of the word . . . can have no possible
influence in producing a moral change in their hearts.'—
Regeneration consists in giving or planting in the heart
a new spiritual taste or relish, (i.e. . . . a spirit of be-

nevolence or preparation of heart to be benevolent to being *simply considered*)—this change is not wro't by the instrumentality of light, or by any means whatever." In this change "an entirely new taste is given for moral beauty . . . which never was or could be seen or tasted before, in the least degree.—Nothing that simple intellect is capable of, can give the idea of any thing properly moral" (p. 23).

In answer to the doctrine that the simple intellect "is incapable of apprehending moral beauty, Hart replied that "the intellect is the leading faculty which constitutes us moral and accountable creatures" (p. 35). And in a general criticism of the ideas of Edwards, he said, "This scheme of doctrines tends to destroy true virtue and real religion: It represents virtue as an unnatural thing, places it on a false and indefensible foundation, and pours contempt upon it, by representing its true beauty, and moral excellencies as of the very same sort with the beauty of material things" (p. 37).

Since Hart rejected the Edwardian conception of true virtue, he had a rather generous estimate of the value of *"that defective sort of virtue which is observable in many men, who are not truly religious."* "Writers are divided in their sentiments concerning actions of this kind," he observed. "Some are disposed to allow them to be virtuous to some degree. Others say there is nothing in them that does at all partake of the nature of true virtue. This is Mr. Edwards's sentiment. Some others go farther and say they are perfect sins."

Hart, on account of his belief in the moral sense, agreed with those who thought that the "defective sort of virtue" is "virtuous in some degree." " 'Tis undeniably true in fact," he said, "that natural conscience and the moral sense, have a very considerable influence in many men, who are not truly religious, in restraining them from many sins, and engaging them to practise many

189

duties: Their hearts, in many instances, concur, in some degree, with the moral sense of their minds. A sense of equity, of moral honour, of gratitude, a spirit of benevolence, compassion, &c. and some kind of regard to God, influence them to do many worthy deeds" (p. 48).

This controversy was temporarily brought to a close in Hemmenway's *Remarks on Mr. Hopkins's Answer to a Vindication,* published in 1774. Hemmenway observed that "certain strange notions which have been lately broached among us . . . have of late been more sinking into disrepute" and he regretted that some men "had been spending the strength of their minds and vigor of their spirits, on these uncouth excrescences." He thought that Edwards, by his inclination "to resolve all the natural affections into self love," had been led into many mistakes in his philosophy of human nature and that Hopkins had repeated his errors. He also thought that Edwards' doctrines of moral inability and of the will were confused and that Hopkins' were even worse.

With this contribution by Hemmenway, the pre-revolutionary controversy over the nature of virtue came to an end.

The situation at the beginning of the Revolution, however, provided a new opportunity for Hopkins to make a political proposal based on his doctrine of benevolence. In 1776, while the Second Continental Congress was in session, he published *A Dialogue concerning the Slavery of the Africans; Shewing it to Be the Duty and Interest of the American States to Emancipate All their African Slaves.* Calling on Congress to make a declaration in favor of emancipation, he based his opposition to slavery on two grounds: (1) it was contrary to the principle of freedom which the Americans had been asserting, and (2) it was contrary to the Christian doctrine of benevolence. Later in publications and in work with organizations Hopkins continued his anti-slavery activity. On this account he incurred the enmity of some of Newport's most prominent families, whose social position was based on wealth gained from the slave trade.

The controversy over the nature of virtue, as over some other theological topics, was interrupted by the Revolution but was resumed shortly after military operations were concluded.

In 1782 David Tappan, later Professor of Divinity at Harvard, published *The Character and Best Exercises of Unregenerate Sinners Set in a Scriptural Light,* in which he stated the doctrine that "Persons in a state of unrenewed nature may perform some things which are their duty, or which in some respects are truly right" (p. 7). Speaking of the ability of the unregenerate to make right choices, Tappan said that "his moral sense also may so strongly reprobate his present vicious affections and practices as highly unreasonable and deformed, and recommend the contrary as so fit and beautiful, as to inspire real and strong desires to be delivered from the one and restored to the other—for as there is a natural beauty in virtue, distinct from spiritual holy beauty, and a correspondent deformity in vice; so there is in the minds of sinners in general a moral sense or taste, which immediately approves and is pleased with the former, but views the latter with disgust" (p. 47).

Tappan was answered by Samuel Spring in *A Friendly Dialogue . . . between Philalethes and Toletus, upon the Nature of Virtue* (1784). In objection to Tappan's estimate of the moral sense, Spring, who had obviously adopted the views of Edwards and Hopkins, asserted: "Now, Sir, please to remember, that the moral sense you have put upon the carpet, cannot be an exercise of the heart. For it has been abundantly proved, that the heart of the sinner is nothing but positive sinfulness: it has also been proved . . . that the human heart is the

191

only seat of moral exercises. By the moral sense, then, you must intend, that class of exercises of the moral agent which are purely intellectual. It must be an exercise of the head, and not of the heart" (p. 144).

Tappan answered Spring's charge that the moral sense is merely an "exercise of the head" in *Two Friendly Letters from Toletus to Philalethes*. "For," he said, "however confident you are, that the moral sense is purely intellectual, yet our daily consciousness and the reasonings of the best writers, prove that it implies some *taste*, which is gratified with the contemplation of right characters and actions, and displeased with the contrary. That pleasure or remorse which we naturally feel in reflecting on our own right or wrong conduct, is a daily experimental proof of such a taste: for as Pleasure is nothing but the gratification of some taste with a suitable object; so remorse is only disgust at something which is disagreeable or opposite to some feeling or affection of the heart. The moral sense then, is a cordial as well as intellectual exercise" (p. 103).

Thinking that Spring and others like him held incorrect conceptions of human nature, Tappan advised them to "read on a larger scale." The authors he recommended were Bishop Butler, Francis Hutcheson, Jonathan Edwards, and Moses Hemmenway.

Spring, however, answered Tappan in *Moral Disquisitions* (1789), in which he relied mainly on Calvinistic doctrine of the Hopkinsian variety. Edwards had written his *Nature of True Virtue* in relation to the doctrine of total depravity, and Spring introduced this doctrine into his reply to Tappan. "If," he said, "sinners are totally depraved, Mr. T's theory is totally groundless." And he declared that Tappan "obviously departs from the first and most capital principle of Calvinism, and adopts the reasoning of uniform Arminians." Spring was dissatisfied because some professed Calvinists were inconsistent with respect to the doctrine of depravity because they believed there could be some merit in the acts of the unregenerate. There was, however, he thought, one school of Calvinistic thought which avoided this inconsistency. "It is evident," he said, "that Hopkinsian sentiments are only the genuine, flourishing and fruitful branches of the Calvinistic tree. For we plead that there is no duty in the actions of sinners, because they are totally depraved. As total depravity, therefore, is the great pillar in Calvinistic doctrine there is no more difference between Calvinists and Hopkinsians, than there is between a tree and its branches or between first principles and consequences" (pp. 47-48).

Because of this reasoning from first principles to consequences there was more philosophical method and philosophical content in the writings of Edwards and the New Divinity school, especially Bellamy and Hopkins, than in the writings of any other theologians of the period. Edwards had correctly anticipated that his *Freedom of the Will* would be criticized because of his use of metaphysics, and the opposition to the New Divinity all along had been partly to the methods of reasoning employed by its proponents.

Before the Revolution, Hopkins had presented his several publications, no one of which contained the total body of his theology. Since then he had labored at an elaborate and logically organized exposition of his ideas. This he published in 1793 as a two volume work of over 1,200 pages entitled *A System of Doctrines Contained in Divine Revelation.*

This book was promptly criticized by Samuel Langdon, President of Harvard, in *Remarks on the Leading Sentiments in the Rev'd Dr. Hopkins's System of Doctrines* (1794). Langdon expressed the same objections that had previously appeared in the controversial publications relating to the New Divinity. In accounting for Hopkins' errors Langdon said: "Few of our systems of divinity have yet been quite free from a mixture of . . . philosophy; and very unhappily for the church, it has lately been revived by the writings of some learned and pious ministers. Among these it may be regretted that Dr. Hopkins now appears one of the foremost. He certainly reasons on several doctrinal articles in a metaphysical way, and so endeavors to establish some peculiar sentiments different from those hitherto generally received" (p. 7).

VII

NATURAL RELIGION AND OTHER PHASES OF RATIONALISTIC LIBERALISM

While Edwards and his followers were attempting to fortify and strengthen the position of Calvinism, liberal theology was also developing more than ever before. In spite of their rationalistic outlook, however, the liberal divines did not use elaborate philosophical reasoning as Edwards and Hopkins had done. Such a topic as the freedom of the will, for instance, was usually handled rather incidentally in a brief passage. Charles Chauncy had said in answer to Edwards' complaint about the use of philosophy by opponents of the revival: "If no use might be made of *Philosophy,* in explaining the *Scripture,* how monstrous must our Conceptions of the infinite GOD be. . . . We must be allowed the Exercise of our *Reason* (which is but another name for what is here meant by *Philosophy*). . . . If we give up our Understandings, how shall we be able to ascertain the Sense of any one Text of Scripture?" It was in this sense that Chauncy himself and other liberal divines were philosophical.

For a while Jonathan Mayhew, of Boston, was the most conspicuous of the liberal ministers. A leading characteristic of Mayhew's outlook was his confidence in the human intellect. In 1749 Mayhew published a volume entitled *Seven Sermons*. These sermons were devoted to the following propositions:

"1. That there is a natural difference betwixt truth and falsehood, right and wrong.

"2. That men are naturally endowed with faculties proper for discerning these differences.

"3. That men are under obligation to exert these faculties; and to judge for themselves in things of a religious concern" (p. 5).

After arguing that truth and right actually exist, Mayhew refuted the idea of the Pyrrhonists, who admit the existence of truth but contend that men are unable to see it. He made use of John Locke to argue for the trustworthiness of the senses and "the certainty and sufficiency of human knowledge" (p. 37). "Since men are naturally endowed with faculties proper for distinguishing betwixt truth and error, right and wrong, . . . hence it follows, that the doctrine of a total ignorance, and incapacity to judge of moral and religious truths, brought upon Mankind by the apostacy of our *First Parents,* is without foundation." Refusing to accept the doctrine that man's intellect is *totally* depraved and darkened because of Adam's fall, Mayhew said: "How much brighter and more vigorous our intellectual faculties were in *Adam,* six thousand years before we had any existence, I leave others to determine. It is sufficient for my purpose to consider mankind as they are at present, without inquiring what they were before they had any being. And it appears that they have now a natural power to judge what is right and true" (p. 38). On account of his faith in human capacity, Mayhew naturally believed in the right of private judgment in matters of religion. "And indeed," he asserted, "the very mention of articles of *faith established by law,* is as great a solecism as *mathematics established by law"* (p. 84).

Mayhew not only believed that the human intellect is capable of understanding religious truth, but he also thought that men are capable of some necessary moral effort prior to regeneration. In 1755 he said something about this effort in a volume of sermons entitled *On Hearing the Word: On Receiving it with Meekness.* It is, he thought, necessary for one to renounce vice in "all its *grosser forms"* before he can receive the Word "with meekness." "It is not possible for those who are regardless *even* of natural religion . . . ; it is not possible for such abandoned sinners, continuing such, to receive the *revealed* word of God with a proper temper of mind. . . . There is somewhat previously requisite, or preparatory thereto." This means that by their own efforts men must "relinquish their brutal lusts, and all gross immoralities" (p. 61).

Mayhew also saw that his view of human capacity for moral effort was related to the doctrine of free-will. Like most of the liberal theologians, Mayhew refused to argue about this problem at length. He considered it a "perplexing question" in which there is "somewhat, which is evidently *too high* for creatures of such limited faculties. . . . " "And," he said, "if we *exercise ourselves in these things,* I know of no valuable end it can answer—except that of convincing us of our ignorance" (p. 291).

Although Mayhew thought that the problem of the will is insoluble by intellectual means, he said that "In that revelation, with which God has favoured us, it is forever taken for granted, that we have a *self-determining* power; (whatever difficulties may attend this supposition) I mean the power either of accepting the mercy offered us, by complying with the gracious terms of it; or rejecting the counsel of God *against ourselves."* "We

196

must either take up with this simple *scriptural* account of the matter; or else bewilder ourselves with that, both needless, and fruitless inquiry, What determines our will and choice to one side, rather than the other" (p. 292). To explain the possibility of free-will, however, he said, "There is, demonstrably, liberty *somewhere*; in some *One* Being, at least." This being is the First Cause. "To deny to this great First Cause, the power of imparting to his creature a *measure* of freedom; or of making a free creature, who can either chuse and act, or not, within a certain sphere, (how narrow and limited soever that sphere may be) is making much *too free with* Him" (p. 296).

Mayhew also expressed unorthodox views regarding regeneration, grace, and the trinity.

To Andrew Croswell, who was a strict Calvinist, Mayhew's doctrines seemed to be hardly more than those of Natural Religion. He therefore sponsored the publication of a sermon entitled *The Insufficience of Natural Religion,* which had originally been preached in London by Abraham Taylor, and was now "reprinted on the Occasion of Dr. Mayhew's late sermons." In a preface, dated September 5, 1755, Croswell said: "The following Discourse seems to be peculiarly calculated to overturn the false idea of *Natural Religion,* imbibed by *Dr. Clark* . . . and his Disciples; and consequently to crush that *Brood of Errors* which have sprung from it, too many of which are to be found in the beforementioned Sermons. My Heart *burned within me* when I read it; and I doubt not, but being *re-published,* it will serve the Cause of Truth in *New* as well as *Old England* and occasion *many Thanksgivings to God.*"

Since the 1730's Natural Religion had not received much attention in New England religious publications. From 1755 onwards, however, this subject won regular and favorable notice in the Dudleian Lectures delivered at Harvard. According to the terms of the founder of the lectureship, the purpose of the first of the lectures and each fourth one thereafter was "to prove, explain or shew the proper use and improvement of the principles of Natural Religion." Unlike Croswell, who deplored the influence of Natural Religion, the ministers who delivered these lectures showed the merits and use of Natural Religion. They always, however, pointed out its limitations and showed how it had to be supplemented and reinforced by revelation. Since Natural Religion was supposed to be based on reason without the aid of revelation, the expositions of the subject necessarily contain a good deal that is of a philosophical nature, pertaining especially to the nature of man and to ethics, and express the ideas of the liberal group, differing sharply, in most cases, from those of traditional Calvinists and of Edwards and his followers.

The first of the Dudleian lectures on Natural Religion, delivered in 1755, was not published. The second one, entitled *Natural Religion as Distinguished from Revealed,* delivered in 1759, was by Ebenezer Gay of Hingham, one of the distinguished members of the liberal group. Referring to the lecture of his predecessor, Gay said, in announcing his own topic: "The Belief of God's Existence is most essentially fundamental to all Religion, and having been at the first of the *Dudleian* Lectures established; the moral Obligation which it induceth upon the Nature of Man may be the subject of our present Inquiry" (p. 1).

Natural Religion Gay defined as "that which bare Reason discovers and dictates." Elaborating on this further, he said: "THAT *Religion is, in some measure, discoverable by the Light, and practicable to the Strength of Nature;* and is so far called *Natural* by Divines and learned men. The Religion which is possible to be discovered by the Light, and practis'd by the Power of

198

Nature, consists in rend'ring all those inward and outward Acts of Respect, Worship and Obedience unto God, which are suitable to the Excellence of his all-perfect Nature. . . . And in yielding to our Fellow-Men that Regard, Help and Comfort, which their partaking of the same Nature, and living in Society with us, give them a Claim to" (p. 7).

Gay, in considering the natural capacities of men, argued that they are able not only to know what their duties are, but also to perform them. "There is doing as well as knowing, by Nature, the Things contained in the Law of it. Knowing them is but in order to the doing them. And the Capacity to know them would be in vain . . . if there was no Ability to do them." This ability to do his duty, Gay thought, means that man must have freedom of the will. "Whoever observes the divine Workmanship in human Nature, and takes a Survey of the Powers and Faculties with which it is endowed, must needs see that it was designed and framed for the Practice of Virtue: That man is not merely so much lumpish Matter, or a *mechanical Engine,* that moves only in the Direction of an impelling force; but that he hath a principle of Action within himself and is an Agent in the strict and proper sense of the Word. The special Endowment of his Nature, which constitutes him such, is the Power of Self-determination, or Freedom of Choice; his being possessed of which is as self-evident, as the Explanation of the Manner of it's operating, is difficult: He feels himself free to act one Way, or another and as he is capable of distinguishing between different Actions, of the moral Kind; so he is likewise capable of chusing which he will do, and which leave undone." Then, apparently having in mind the moral sense, Gay added, "Further to qualify our Nature for virtuous or religious Practice . . . the Author of it hath annexed a secret Joy or Complacence of Mind to

199

such Practice, and as sensible a Pain or Desplicence to the contrary'' (p. 12).

In attempting to account for the natural moral preferences of men, Gay used a scientific parallel. ''THERE may be,'' he said, ''something in the intelligent moral World analogous to Attraction in the Material System—something that inclines Man toward God, the Centre of their Perfection, and consummate Object of their Happiness; and which, if its energy were not obstructed, would as certainly procure such Regularity in the states and actions of all intelligent beings in the spiritual World, as that of Attraction doth in the Positions and Motions of all the Bodies in the material world'' (p. 12).

Gay's high estimate of men's capacities was hardly in accordance with the Calvinistic doctrine of total depravity, but it was not the same as the view of those, the Deists, for instance, who completely ignored the results of the fall of man. ''REASON, as well as Revelation,'' Gay said, ''teacheth us, that in it's original Constitution, and as it came out of the Hands of a good Creator, must be perfect in its Kind, and that it since, by our Abuse of it, is wofully impaired. . . . Some appear to have an extravagantly high Opinion, and others a too debasing Notion of human Nature, even in it's lapsed Estate: There are still in it, as received by Derivation from Apostate Parents, some *legible Characters, Outlines,* and *Lineaments* of its Beauty; some *magnificent Ruins,* which shew what it had been, enough to demonstrate the original Impression of the divine Image and Law. It is, however disorder'd and debilitated, a rational Nature, capable of religious Knowledge and Practice'' (pp. 26-27).

The idea that human nature had been impaired but not completely vitiated as a result of Adam's fall was common to the rationalistic liberals among the New

England divines and was largely responsible for their deviation from Calvinism on many other points.

In the next Dudleian lecture on Natural Religion, however, there was more emphasis on depravity than in Gay's. It was delivered in 1763 by Peter Clark, who had previously, in 1758-60, written four pamphlets on the Calvinistic side in a controversy over the doctrine of original sin. In this lecture, entitled *Man's Dignity and Duty as a Reasonable Creature; and his Insufficiency as a Fallen Creature,* Clark defined Natural Religion as consisting "in such laws, or rules of moral conduct, as are founded on deductions from principles of meer natural reason relative to divinity and morality." "The practice of it consists in the due observance of those rules." It is "the excellency of natural religion, that it hath its foundation in the rational nature of man, and is therefore stable, fixed and indispensable. . . . it is fundamental to all civil order, the welfare of society and laws of government" (pp. 3-4).

Less sanguine than Gay about man's present capacity for moral conduct, Clark said of natural religion: "Nevertheless, if we consider it, with respect to the great end of all religion, the guiding men to God as their ultimate, supream happiness, it must be confess'd, that the meer religion of nature, which was calculated for a state of innocent, uncorrupt nature, and could serve to this end only in such a state, is now, in the present degenerate state of mankind, in many respects defective, and insufficient to conduct him to his great end" (p. 4).

The lecture as a whole was devoted mainly to two doctrines:

"I. That there is a matter of duty expected and required of man, purely as he is a reasonable creature" (p. 7).

"II. That men do generally fail in those duties which

201

their own reason duly attended to would lead them to the observance of" (p. 26).

The speaker picked out one particular duty—that of repentance—to show that "Both natural and revealed religion agree in requiring this duty of sinners." But "natural religion is defective, as it cannot furnish a sinner wth sufficient aids and inducements to repentance." Since "the distempered nature of a sinner cannot heal itself by any power it is possessed of, the cure must be derived from a supernatural influence. The light and power of reason is too much darkened and debilitated . . . to be able to throw off vicious customs and reform the heart . . . " (p. 31).

In other discourses not primarily devoted to the subject, Natural Religion was occasionally commented upon. Samuel West, in an ordination sermon, preached in 1764, pointing out the danger of two extremes, said: "Where the doctrines of meer natural religion are insisted upon to the neglect of the peculiar doctrines of revelation, we can at most expect to find only a few fashionable civil gentlemen, but destitute of real piety. As on the other hand, where the distinguishing doctrines of Christianity alone are insisted upon, we shall find that men are very apt to run into enthusiasm. A true gospel minister should seek to avoid both extreams. When he insists on moral vertues, he should enforce them on Christian motives" (p. 20).

As was seen in the case of Mayhew and Gay, one of the characteristics of the liberal ministers was a belief in the capacity of men to perform duties which are both meritorious and efficacious in relation to salvation. Charles Chauncy, who had published only occasional sermons since the revival, published a volume in 1765 entitled *Twelve Sermons*, in which he presented a highly favorable view of human nature. The theme was "justification by faith," and Chauncy, like the orthodox, maintained that justification is "impossible by the Works of the Law." Because of his conception of human nature, however, he placed a high value on effort, as he explained in a sermon entitled "Human Endeavours, in the use of Means, the way in which faith is obtained." "Another thing I desire may be . . . taken notice of is," he said, "that sinners, tho' destitute of the faith that is justifying, have yet other principles in their nature, that are capable of giving rise to a great variety of actions, both inward and outward; and this, as it respects religion, and the salvation of their souls." Then, describing men's intellectual processes in terms of the psychology of John Locke, Chauncy said: "As intelligent moral beings, they are endowed not only with perceptive powers, rendering them capable of admitting ideas into their minds, the original materials of all knowledge; they are endowed not only with the faculty of retaining these ideas there, of attending to them, of comparing them one with another, of judging of their agreement or disagreement, and, in these ways, of discovering a great variety of interesting truths: I say, not only are they endowed with these capacities, but with liberty of choice, and a power, in consequence hereof, of acting this way or that, without hindrance or restraint."

Like Gay and other liberals, Chauncy did not believe that depravity was total. "Sinners, notwithstanding all their depravity and guilt, are," he said, "still capable of thinking, reasoning, considering, reflecting; they are still capable of chusing some things in preference to others, and of ordering their conduct conformably to such choice. . . ."

"A large fund . . . is here opened for human endeavours, from other principles besides that of faith which is justifying." Sinners who cannot act from faith "may yet do a great deal from other principles planted in their nature" (pp. 202-204).

The liberal ministers of this period, in general, not only held favorable views of the nature and capacity of man but also amiable sentiments about the attributes of God. To the Calvinists, God's chief attribute was His absolute sovereignty. One of the chief instances of His exercise of sovereignty was the election of some men to damnation and others to salvation. To the liberals this concept of God's sovereignty was abhorrent.

In England the most notable exposition of a changed conception of God had been Samuel Clarke's *Discourses on the Being and Attributes of God* (1705-1706). Clarke maintained that God's sovereignty is limited by wisdom, justice, and mercy. In New England the influence of Clarke's view is most clearly apparent in Jonathan Mayhew. For Thanksgiving observance of 1762 Mayhew preached *Two Sermons on the Nature, Extent and Perfection of the Divine Goodness*. In treating the divine attributes he said: "The eternity, immensity and immutability of God; his perfect purity, holiness, primitive justice; tho' all adorable attributes, yet being considered independent of his bounty, clemency and mercy, rather astonish and confound, than please or delight us, by appearing amiable to us. . . . Whereas, being considered as inseparably connected with goodness, which is equally essential to the divine nature, those otherwise formidable attributes, are, in a great degree, stripped of their terror." And, regarding the divine goodness, Mayhew added, "that it would be very *unnatural,* as well as impious in any, to restrain or confine it, in a manner not warranted either by reason or the holy scriptures" (p. 18).

A similar concept of God was stated by Andrew Eliot in *A Discourse on Natural Religion,* the Dudleian lecture of 1771. Eliot said that "though we are obliged to think and speak of . . . distinct attributes of God, there is but one principle of action in him; all may be reduced to boundless intelligence or wisdom." In amplification of this he quoted from William Wollaston's *The Religion of Nature Delineated* that this "wisdom" is "Divine Reason, which, as it exerts itself upon this or that occasion, is by us variously denominated Justice, Mercy, Truth, or whatever else goes to contribute moral perfection, or perfect moral conduct" (pp. ix-x).

The benevolence of God was given a special emphasis in a pamphlet entitled *A Sermon on Natural Religion. By a Natural Man* (1771), the author of which was presumably a layman. The writer defined "a natural man" as "a person who directs all his actions by the dictates of reason, and who contemplates the works of nature with an awful and reverent admiration." "Natural religion is," he said, "a worship and contemplation of an only infinite and eternal being, and of his attributes, as far as human nature is capable of the investigation of them." In his investigation of the divine attributes, the natural man finds "that his God must be all goodness, and consequently that he cannot decree any one to everlasting damnation, as he formed every thing for the best in its kind" (p. 8).

The Dudleian lecture of 1775, delivered by Samuel Langdon, President of Harvard, was entitled *The Coincidence of Natural with Revealed Religion.* Langdon followed the usual pattern in describing the nature, merits, and deficiencies of Natural Religion. One of his reasons for the desirability of revelation is, however, different from those given by his predecessors in the lectureship. If man's reason had remained in its perfect state it "might be supposed capable of arriving at the knowledge of *One true God,* and deducing from thence a compleat system of natural religion." Previous lecturers had apparently assumed that this knowledge could be readily acquired. Langdon, however, drawing an analogy with the development of science, thought that the formation of a "complete system of natural religion" would have been a long and slow process. "Yet," he said, "it can hardly be conceived, according to our experience of the labor of searching out truth, that the human mind, in its utmost strength, could by one glance of thought discover all the essential characters of the Deity, or the proper acts of worship and obedience which he requires. We might as well affirm that unimpaired reason must naturally, at the first view of the heavenly bodies, have a clear knowledge of their magnitudes, distances, and revolutions: or by looking round on the earth, immediately be acquainted with the innumerable gradations of animal life, and vegetable productions and Fossils of all forms and uses. In such limited beings as man, there cannot be an instantaneous knowledge of things, especially such as are sublime and remote from sense; the discovery of one truth leads to another, and by constant progress we perfect every theory."

"Therefore it may justly be questioned whether, if man at his first creation, furnished with the strongest mental powers, and continuing innocent and free from any bias against the knowledge of God, had been left to himself entirely, to form his notions of a Deity, merely by his own reflections, without any supernatural revelation, it would not have cost the labor of Ages to demonstrate a true System of religion, as it has really taken near six thousand years to search out the laws of the material system, and bring natural philosophy to its present perfection" (p. 11).

Obviously, supernatural revelation was the only solution of this problem.

The Dudleian lecture of 1779, entitled *Natural Religion Aided by Revelation and Perfected by Christianity*, was delivered by Gad Hitchcock. The ordinary idea was that the principles of natural religion are discovered by reason. Hitchcock's conception of the role of reason was slightly different. "I am inclined to think," he said, "that natural religion is not so properly defined to be that, which mankind have, or might come to the knowledge of, meerly by the strength of unassisted reason; but as that, which reason sees to be right, and feels the force of, when it is known." Hitchcock, like Langdon, believed that achievement of correct religious ideas would have been much delayed if man had received no divine aid. "Reason, properly employed," he said, "will make very great discoveries, and by attending to the constitution and order of things, be led up to their cause. This notwithstanding, had the immediate posterity of Adam received no light from him, or communication from the Deity, their progress in moral science would undoubtedly have been very slow" (pp. 15-16).

To account for man's slowness in the acquisition of knowledge, Hitchcock made use of the epistemology of John Locke. "The opinion of innate ideas and principles, which prevailed for so long a time, is now almost universally given up; and that of the human mind receiving them afterwards distinct and simple; comparing, compounding and disposing of them, together with the perception of those operations, is adopted in its room, as the original of knowledge" (p. 20). This was, Hitchcock thought, the way in which even Adam had gained his knowledge. The traditional idea was that Adam had perfect knowledge which had been infused into him instantaneously. He thought that although Adam had acquired his knowledge gradually, he had, before the fall, learned faster than men have done afterwards and had also received some direct aid from his Creator. In defense of his idea that Adam had acquired his knowledge in the ordinary manner, he said: "No doctrine of religion, that I know of, Natural or revealed, would, in any degree, be affected, much less injured by it: It is indisputably more consonant to the subsequent ways of divine providence. We can have no conception of knowledge in man, or indeed in any other creature, but that, which is made up of ideas gradually admitted, and properly ordered by the understanding" (p. 20).

In the part of the lecture devoted to showing the superiority of revealed religion, he made an appeal to the Deists, who, he thought, had themselves profited by the revelation which they repudiated. "It is indeed," he said, "owing in part to the greater improvements, which later ages have made in science and liternature, than former ages had done, that the modern Deists know more, and more they certainly do know than their predecessors, the ancient philosophers. But this is chiefly to be attributed to the advantage of the Christian revelation, which has been a rich blessing, even to those who do not believe in it. One would be ready to imagine that we meet the Deists on their own ground, and give them all their wishes, when we undertake to shew that the Christian revelation is the fulfilment and perfection of the same plan which the Deity has pursued with men from the first; and that the great aim and tendency of it is to give them more just and enlarged notions of the principles, and more strongly to oblige them to the duties of natural religion. Whether this be the case or not, they themselves will allow, is worthy their most serious consideration" (pp. 30-31).

* * * * *

The two most influential features of the liberal religious thought which we have seen developing in the second half of the eighteenth century were the high estimate of the intellectual and moral capacities of men and the emphasis on the benevolent attributes of God.

In the publications of Charles Chauncy issued after the Revolution in which the doctrine of universal salvation is presented, we find the greatest emphasis placed on God's benevolence. The most important of these publications is entitled *The Mystery Hid from Ages and Generations, or, The Salvation of All Men* (1784). The basis of Chauncy's argument is stated in two propositions: (1) "As the First Cause of all things is infinitely benevolent, 'tis not easy to conceive, that he should bring mankind into existence, unless he intended to make them finally happy, and (2) if this was his intention, it cannot well be supposed, as he is infinitely intelligent and wise, that he should be able to project or carry into execution, a scheme that would be ineffectual to secure, sooner or later, the certain accomplishment of it" (p. 1).

Although Chauncy made the divine benevolence the main foundation of his Universalist doctrine, he also thought that man is not sinful enough to be condemned to eternal punishment. This of course meant repudiation of the doctrine of original sin or total depravity. This topic he dealt with in *Five Dissertations on the Scripture Account of the Fall* (1785). He did not deny that there had been a fall nor that it had had an effect on Adam's posterity. This effect was, however, not *total* depravity. "The . . . thing that mankind universally are subject to since the lapse, and in consequence of it, is a STATE OF NATURE LESS PERFECT, than it might otherwise have been" (p. 160). Men are not born in an actual state of sin, but since Adam's human nature has been transmitted to them, "they may come into being with animal tendencies, which may prove the occasion of their sinning themselves" (p. 132).

In the last years of the century the rationalistic spirit was slightly dampened for a while on account of the radical nature of the religious and political thought of the French *philosophes* and other leaders of the French Revolution. The most vigorous religious publications of the late 1780's and the 1790's were denunciations of French "infidelity," which was feared as a subversive influence, fatal to religion, morality and government. Related to these were attacks on Thomas Paine's *Age of Reason* (1792), which, it was feared, was being circulated to assist a scheme of subversion.

One of these alarmists was Timothy Dwight, President of Yale. In a fourth of July sermon entitled *The Duty of Americans at the Present Crisis,* delivered in 1788, Dwight advocated severance of diplomatic relations with France. After describing the opinions and conduct of the French leaders, he asked, "For what end shall we be connected with men of whom this is the character? Is it that we may assume the same character and pursue the same conduct? Is it, that our churches may become temples of reason . . . ? . . . Shall our sons become the disciples of Voltaire . . . ?" (p. 20).

On account of current concern about infidelity the last of the Dudleian lectures delivered in the eighteenth century included an observation for which there had been no occasion in the earlier lectures. This lecture, entitled *A Discourse on Natural Religion,* was delivered in 1799, by John Mellen. "The subject of this Lecture," Mellen said, "assumes a peculiar degree of importance, at the present day, when the foundations of natural as well as revealed religion, are so boldly and virulently attacked, by an impious and atheistical philosophy;—a philosophy which would exalt *nature* to the throne of NATURE's GOD; and which, under the pretext of destroying superstition. and freeing mankind from unreasonable restraints, opens the flood-gates of the vilest passions, levels those barriers, on which the security of the social order essentially depends" (p. 24).

Previous apologists for natural religion had had to defend it against those who had a too low estimate of human reason. In the present situation, as Mellen noted, natural religion was menaced from the other direction —by rationalism which had ended in atheism. In view of this fact it was necessary to defend religion itself, not merely to present the respective merits of natural and revealed religion. Mellen therefore, addressing the Harvard students in his audience, warned against the effects of Atheism as exhibited in recent French history, and then added: "I will appeal to your understandings, and your feelings . . . whether there be not a just foundation for religion, laid in the nature of man; whether the heavens do not declare the existence, and glorious perfections of the Deity; whether the earth be not full of the evidences of his power, wisdom, and goodness: whether he have not shewed us, in the most important instances, even by the light of reason and nature, what is good, and what he requireth of us" (pp. 25-26).

Meanwhile, during the years of excitement and alarm about infidelity, rationalist liberalism had quietly persisted. After the death of Chauncy in 1786, however, it was without impressive spokesmen. Nevertheless, as young men replaced the older ones in the pulpits and membership in the congregations changed with the passing of time, there was a continuity in the doctrinal outlook in both ministers and people in parishes where the liberal doctrines had been preached and accepted. It is for this reason that the transition to Unitarianism in the early nineteenth century was easy and scarcely perceptible in some of the congregations. Although Unitarianism gets its name because of its rejection of the orthodox doctrine of the Trinity, the most important features of the Unitarianism of Eastern Massachusetts are found in other matters, and particularly in two views which were basic to the liberalism of the eighteenth century—the high estimate placed on the intellectual and moral capacities of man and the emphasis on benevolence as the chief attribute of God. Members of the congregations which became Unitarian did not have to adopt these views as new—they already had them. The only change in the shift to Unitarianism was, therefore, in the doctrine which concerned Christ and the atonement, and even this was connected with views concerning God and man. If man was essentially good, as the Unitarians believed, no such drastic measure as the crucifixion of Christ was required for atonement. The orthodox doctrine of atonement, the Unitarians thought, was not only based on a false idea of man's character, but also implied cruelty on the part of God, who, according to the conception they had become accustomed to, was infinitely benevolent.

The Unitarian ministers were not primarily concerned with doctrinal matters, and their reading was devoted to history and literature more than to theology. On account of this fact and because of their generous views of human nature, they contributed to the formation of an intellectual atmosphere which made possible the literary "flowering of New England."

By preparing the way for Unitarianism the eighteenth-century liberals undoubtedly contributed to a trend in religious thought which has had a continuous history until the present time. The direct influence of their writings, however, barely outlasted their own time.

Today the only theologian of the colonial period whose writings exert a direct influence is Jonathan Edwards. Conservative theology is now in the ascendancy, and doctrines derived from Edwards form an integral part of one of the conservative systems of divinity.